KU-061-878

Contents

How to use this book

The Teach Yourself Breakthrough series has a number of features to help you get the most out of reading this book. *Overcome Phobias and Panic Attacks* includes the following boxed features:

 Assess yourself at the start of each chapter.

 Case studies provide a more in-depth introduction to a particular example.

 Key idea boxes distil the most important ideas and thoughts.

 Remember this boxes help you to take away what really matters.

 Mythbuster boxes provide interesting facts and challenge some widely-held beliefs.

 Focus points at the end of each chapter help you to hone in on the core message of each chapter.

Introduction

It is estimated that between three and ten per cent of the population suffer from phobias, most of which are also associated with some form of panic attack. So, if you are reading this because you suffer from a phobia or from panic attacks, you are most certainly not alone. These severe anxiety conditions do not discriminate and can strike anyone, whatever their background. Phobias and panic attacks are not, however, the only form that anxiety disorders can take and some people may have obsessive–compulsive disorder alongside their panic. Sometimes, people can develop a severe anxiety disorder incorporating some or all of these conditions, in response to a traumatic event; this is termed post-traumatic stress disorder.

All of these conditions can be treated and this book guides you through the cognitive behavioural techniques that can be applied using exercises, diaries, self-diagnostic quizzes and other interactive strategies. All the techniques in this book are those that I use with my own clients at my private phobia and panic attack clinic (www.mindtrainingclinic.co.uk) in Manchester, UK. Please note that the diagnostic quizzes should not be used instead of professional diagnosis and also that, in many cases, professional input might be advised (more on this in the first two chapters).

This book is designed to be used in either of two ways depending on your needs. Some readers will prefer to read from cover to cover, while others might feel they only need a few of the chapters. The material is presented in a format to meet both needs, with the aim of making the information accessible to those reading only selected parts, but in a manner that is not too repetitive for readers wanting to engage with the whole book. To this end, where sections are relevant to more than one chapter, rather than repeat them, the reader is given clear cross-references. Sometimes the material is reproduced in more than one chapter for ease, but this is usually for tables or diagrams (which are easily skipped if you are already familiar with them). Sometimes material is presented in more than one chapter, but tailored differently, e.g. 'unhelpful thinking styles' – this key material is used several times in the book, such as within the section on anxiety conditions in Chapter 3, for social phobia in Chapter 6 and depression in Chapter 10. The material is presented with different emphasis each time, so merely referring the reader back to a generic description of unhelpful thinking styles would not have been as useful.

Whichever way you use this book (and 'use' is probably the right word here, as it is designed as a practical book to be worked through rather than just read), you should find all you need to learn more about what causes your anxiety condition and how to go about treating it or accessing the right professional help. To get the most out of the book, try the suggested exercises, workplans etc. so that you can tailor the material for your own needs.

Overcoming phobias, panic attacks and other anxiety conditions is possible, even if you have lived with the condition for many years. The methods in this book have been tried and tested at my clinic, and I have not had any failures yet; they only 'don't work' on the rare occasion when a client decides not to follow the suggested strategies. The strategies are designed to enable you to go at your own, graduated pace and should ensure that you are never facing situations which are too stressful for you.

So, good luck, stay with the programme and look forward to a new life. I'd love to hear your success stories; you can contact me via my website (www.mindtrainingclinic.co.uk).

1

Introduction to phobias

In this chapter you will learn:

- ▶ *What phobias are*
- ▶ *The difference between phobias and fear*
- ▶ *About the symptoms of phobias*
- ▶ *What help is available and how to access that help*

What are phobias?

Most people, when asked what a phobia is, will probably talk about fears or even intense dislikes. People with spider phobias, for example, are thought to be very scared of the multi-legged insects and/or to dislike them passionately.

Yet a phobia is much more than a simple fear or strong dislike of something. In the current economic climate, you might fear losing your job, but that doesn't make you phobic about it. I might strongly dislike olives (in fact, I hate them) but again, that doesn't make me phobic about olives.

What then, distinguishes a phobia from a mere fear or dislike of something? To be called a 'phobia' most practitioners follow the diagnostic guidelines set in the *Diagnostic and Statistical Manual* (known in the trade as DSM-IV, for the 4th edition of the manual) which is published by the American Psychiatric Association (1994). These guidelines point out that in order to be classified as a phobia, four conditions must be met:

▶ A marked and persistent fear that is excessive or unreasonable, cued by the presence or anticipation of a specific object or situation.

- Exposure to this stimulus almost invariably provokes an immediate anxiety response, which may take the form of a panic attack.

- The person recognizes that the fear is excessive or unreasonable.

- The phobic response interferes significantly with the person's normal routine or social activities.

Remember this

Phobias differ from fears in that they are severe, excessive, persistent, provoke intense anxiety responses and interfere with normal day-to-day life.

This means that the phobic individual experiences an extreme (and unwanted) fear or excessive anxiety when faced with the object of their phobia and that even thinking about the object or situation will bring on intense anxiety. The anxiety felt has to be *persistent* for it to be classed as a phobia – in other words, if you are sometimes afraid of heights but sometimes OK, this wouldn't be classed as a phobia. The severe anxiety felt is often in the form of a panic attack which is why phobias and panic attacks are so closely linked. (There will be more on panic attacks in Chapter 2.) The fear is also unreasonable in that it can't be explained.

All this differs from a normal fear response where the fear or anxiety is an appropriate response to a threatening (or apparently threatening) situation. Thus, if a wild Rottweiler lunges at me, my fear and its corresponding reactions (such as increased heart rate, faster breathing etc.) are perfectly normal and justified because the dog is threatening me. In fact, it is worth pointing out that not only is this fear normal and justified, it can actually be helpful as it activates the automatic fight-or-flight response which provides our body and brain with the resources to escape (or stay and fight). This is explained in more detail later in this chapter and also in Chapter 3.

If this fear later *generalizes* so that I exhibit the same reaction when seeing a small Yorkshire Terrier across the road, then the fear becomes unreasonable as this dog is not likely to be a real threat (although Yorkies can be quite ferocious little things!).

Quiz: Which of these reactions is a normal fear, and which is a phobic reaction?

	Normal fear?	Phobic reaction?
1 Avoiding going on holiday abroad so as to avoid flying		
2 Feeling acute fear when the plane you are flying in experiences turbulence		
3 Getting nervous before giving a presentation and feeling a bit sick		
4 Making excuses to avoid giving presentations at work		
5 Avoiding going in a very small and old-fashioned lift in a warehouse		
6 Avoiding going in any lifts		
7 Pulling your kids away from a Dobermann and crossing the road to avoid it		
8 Not taking your kids to the park in case you encounter a dog		
9 Dreading going to the dentist for dental treatment		
10 Avoiding going to the dentist for dental treatment		
11 Screaming when you see a spider		
12 Avoiding several rooms in the house in case of spiders		

Obviously, 1, 4, 6, 8, 10 and 12 are the phobic responses!

The DSM-IV criteria also demand that the phobic person recognizes that their fear is excessive or unreasonable. This is an interesting concept – can someone have a phobia without realizing that they do? It is here that I disagree slightly with the DSM guidelines, in that I am aware there are plenty of people out there who are in denial about their problem (although perhaps this denial hides a deep-seated acknowledgement that they do have a problem). In fact, it is often the case that partners, spouses, family members etc. will be the ones seeking help, while the affected individuals deny that there is anything untoward (see Mike's case study later in this chapter). Interestingly, this is often the case with obsessive–compulsive disorder, which is covered in Chapter 9.

Mythbuster

It is often thought that phobic people think their fears are entirely reasonable, but in actual fact, most realize that there is no logical reason to fear the source of their phobia (e.g. they know that the spider is unlikely to harm them).

This issue of acknowledgement of the problem, together with the DSM's fourth criterion, will be discussed in the section on 'Does your phobia need treating?', later in this chapter.

Self-diagnostic quiz: Do you have a phobia?
While not a replacement for professional diagnosis, this quiz can be a useful indicator of whether or not you have a phobia. How much do you agree with the following statements?

	1 Strongly disagree	2 Disagree	3 Agree	4 Strongly agree
When I see the source of my fear I get very anxious.				
When I think about the source of my fear I get very anxious.				
If I imagine touching or interacting with the source of my phobia my anxiety grows.				
I know that, logically, there is no real reason to be so anxious about or fearful of the object or situation.				
I cannot control my reactions to my feared object or situation.				
I am afraid that my anxiety will be so great that something will happen to me (e.g. I might faint, vomit etc.).				
The anxiety I feel is so great that I avoid situations where I might encounter the source of my fear.				
I always have the same or similar reactions to my feared object or situation.				
My fear is limiting my life in that I can't do things that I want to do.				
I know that the object of my fear isn't going to harm me but I still can't help getting anxious.				

The more 3s or 4s, the more likely it is that you have a phobia. However, see also the 'Does your phobia need treating?' quiz later in this chapter for more on the degree and severity of your phobia.

Key idea

The first step to beating a phobia is to recognize and acknowledge that you have it.

TYPES OF PHOBIA

Although these will be dealt with in greater detail in Chapters 6 and 7, the different types of phobia that can occur are worth mentioning here (see Figure 1.1).

Phobias can be classified into two broad types:

▶ specific or simple phobias;

▶ complex phobias (e.g. social phobia or agoraphobia – more on these in Chapter 6).

Specific phobias can be further classified into four main categories which are:

▶ animal phobias (fear of animals or creatures);

▶ environmental phobias (fear of environmental events such as thunder, lightning, heights, the dark etc.);

▶ medical phobias (fear of blood, injections, vomiting, injury etc.);

▶ situational phobias (fear of certain situations such as crowded places, public transport, flying, driving etc.).

These will be expanded on in greater detail in Chapter 7.

Remember this

If a phobia is such that it is hard to leave the house or interact with people, it may be a complex phobia such as social phobia or agoraphobia (see Chapter 6 for more on complex phobias).

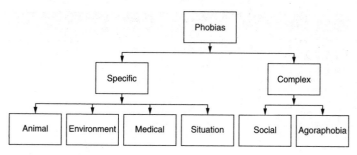

Figure 1.1 Types of phobia

Symptoms of phobias

By now, you will probably have a pretty good idea of what a phobia is and what it is not, but it is useful to identify the actual symptoms of a phobia. Many people who suffer these symptoms don't realize that they are symptoms of a phobia; indeed, it is very common for sufferers to believe that they are having (or going to have) a heart attack or have some undiagnosed medical condition. It is always advisable to see a medical practitioner to rule out the very rare chance that there is an underlying medical explanation for your symptoms – once this possibility has been eliminated, the chances are that symptoms experienced are directly caused by the reaction to the phobia.

The following is a list of common symptoms that often occur when encountering the object of a phobia. It is useful to indicate how often you experience each symptom.

Quiz: Symptoms of phobia – how often do you experience these symptoms when encountering the source of your phobia?

	1 Very often	2 Often	3 Sometimes	4 Rarely
Hyperventilating				
Palpitations				
Breathlessness				
Rapid heartbeat				
Sweating				
Dry mouth				
Difficulty swallowing				

Continued

	1 Very often	2 Often	3 Sometimes	4 Rarely
Choking sensation				
Feeling faint				
Nausea				
Dizziness				
Chest pain				
Trembling/shaking				

Remember this

It is worth pointing out that, while these symptoms feel really awful for the sufferer, they are not dangerous.

It is important to understand why these symptoms occur; this understanding is the basis for treating a phobia and will be explained briefly here and expanded upon in later chapters.

Key idea

Understanding the mechanism behind the symptoms that sufferers experience when faced with their phobia is very important for them to realize that their reactions are normal and not harmful.

Quite simply, a severe phobic reaction is a classic 'stress' reaction. A stress reaction is the 'fight-or-flight' reaction mentioned earlier and is designed to help our bodies prepare for action when faced with a threat. For our ancestors, threats usually required either a fight response (staying and fighting a ferocious lion or even a ferocious fellow human) or running away fast (when it is clear that said lion or human is likely to win the fight). To achieve either aim, they needed energy – particularly in their legs and arms (to run or fight) and their brain (to think clearly).

Energy is provided in the form of oxygen-rich blood. In order to get that oxygen-rich blood to the limbs and brain quickly, our heart pumps faster, our breathing rate increases (to breathe more oxygen in) and blood is diverted from less essential functions (like digesting food and saliva production) to the limbs/brain (see Chapter 3 for more on this). These reactions explain most of the physical symptoms experienced.

Mythbuster

Phobic people suffering extreme panic often believe that they might vomit, collapse or have a heart attack. These things rarely happen.

Quiz: The physical symptoms are often accompanied by emotional symptoms too. How often do you experience the following symptoms?

	1 Very often	2 Often	3 Sometimes	4 Rarely
Feeling of panic				
An intense need to escape from the situation that is producing these feelings and symptoms				
Feeling detached from yourself or 'out of it'				
Fear that you are going to die, faint or have a heart attack				

These feelings are often so intense that sufferers will do anything to avoid their recurrence – which is why phobias can impact their lives so greatly.

Remember this

The symptoms of a phobia are often so unpleasant that sufferers go to great lengths to avoid experiencing them. This means that their phobia often ends up controlling their life, determining where they go, what they do etc.

Does your phobia need treating?

The first three of the DSM-IV criteria (see previous section) might lead to a diagnosis of 'phobia' in theory but, in practice, a phobia only becomes a significant problem when the fourth criterion is also present. Thus, this last criterion, for me in my (private) practice, is the crux; I get many people in social situations telling me about their 'phobia' and asking whether it needs treating. The defining issue is whether the problem limits their life, whether it stops them doing things they ordinarily would do. Thus, for example, James might be 'phobic' of tunnels, but is usually able to manage his life perfectly well without venturing in one. Sue told me that she was 'phobic' about snakes, but as she never expects to encounter them on a day-to-day basis, this does not affect her normal life and thus does not need treating. (See case study below for an example of a problem phobia.)

Case study: Batya's Underground/Tube phobia

Batya had been afraid of going in the Underground (subway/tube) all her life. She would never, ever travel on an underground train, despite living in London where transportation by 'Tube' was the norm to get around. She got the phobia from her mum who was once stuck on a Tube train when it broke down and afterwards would never use the Tube or take her kids on a Tube train. Batya had three siblings, all of whom avoided the Underground. When Batya rang me, she was 24 years old and had successfully managed to avoid using the Underground all her life. She would travel by bus and, although it was slower, this rarely presented a major problem. She did avoid one or two situations where the bus wasn't a viable option – for example, she had a friend who lived near a Tube station but not near a convenient bus route, so she overcame this problem by arranging to meet the friend elsewhere. She managed her phobia in secret – no one (except her family) knew the real reason for her avoidance of the Underground as she felt ashamed of her problem.

Batya is a clear example of someone whose phobia was in control and who could manage her life without treating it. Because she could manage, she had no motivation for getting rid of her phobia. Until the day she was offered the job of her dreams – on a Tube line but not on a bus route. It would take her 40 minutes to get into her new office every day if she used the Tube – but 2½ hours if she used the bus/walking option. She suddenly realized that she had to cure her phobia – fast. She couldn't spend 5 hours commuting to her new job – in fact, the job also entailed going out and about to other businesses for meetings etc, so in reality, she would be likely to have to use the Tube several times a day, as buses took too long and taxis were too expensive.

Now, her problem had turned into a phobia that needed treating!

There are generally three stages to seeking help for a phobia:

▶ Stage 1

Acknowledgement that there is a problem. The DSM-IV guidelines (see earlier) go so far as to suggest that without acknowledgement of the problem, a fear cannot be classified as a phobia. Certainly, unless someone realizes that they have a problem, they won't seek help and, as mentioned earlier, many people remain in denial for quite a long time before accepting that their problem is serious enough to need help.

Why then do many people refuse to acknowledge their problem? In my experience, there are a range of reasons:

▶ People are ashamed or embarrassed to think that they might have a 'mental health' problem.

▶ They feel that they should be able to sort this out themselves.

▶ They get so used to adapting their life around their problem (e.g. avoiding lifts) that they don't realize they are doing so.

▶ They don't see the phobia as a problem because they can manage perfectly well by avoiding the source of their fear (as Batya, in the case study above, did before she got her new job).

This denial can go on for years and, quite often, it is other people close to the sufferer who acknowledge the problem first and try to encourage them to seek help (see Mike's case study later in this chapter).

▶ Stage 2

Seeking self-help. Here the sufferer realizes that they have a problem and that they need to get some outside input. They are not yet ready to seek professional help for a number of reasons:

▶ They don't think their problem is so bad that it needs professional help.

▶ They are embarrassed or ashamed to go to a 'mental health professional'.

- They are worried that seeing a therapist will go on their medical record and affect employment prospects etc.
- They haven't got time to go to appointments.

Self-help is available in many forms, including books like this, internet advice etc.

▶ Stage 3

This is where professional help is sought either via referral within the NHS from the family doctor or by self-referral to private therapists or trainers. Often a sufferer will have tried the self-help route and either not chosen a good source of self-help for them, or else their problem is so severe that they really need professional input.

If you are reading this book then you are probably in Stage 2 at least but in case you still want to know whether your phobia needs treating, answer the questions in the quiz below.

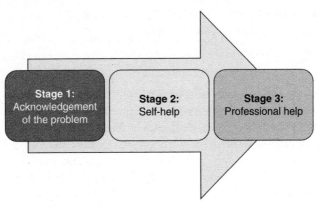

Figure 1.2 Stages of seeking help

Mythbuster

Many phobic sufferers think that they are beyond help or that getting cured will be too uncomfortable. Yet most phobias can be cured relatively quickly and a good practitioner should ensure that the discomfort is never too much too bear.

Quiz: Does your phobia need treating?

	1 Never	2 Sometimes	3 Often	4 Very often
Does your phobia stop you doing things you want to do?				
Does it stop you leading a normal life?				
Does your phobia affect your work or your ability to work?				
Does your phobia affect your social life?				
Are you limited or restricted in where you go because of your phobia?				
Does your phobia affect your quality of life?				

If you score more than 2 on at least three items, then your phobia does need sorting!

Remember this

If your phobia is not significantly restricting your life, you probably won't be motivated to get it treated.

Who gets phobias?

It is thought that 10 to 12 per cent of the population will experience a phobia over the course of their life (Adler and Cook-Nobles, 2011) with figures varying for the different types (see Chapter 6 for further details). It is thought that more women suffer from phobias than men (although this could be because women are more likely to seek professional help for their phobias than men) and that they are more prevalent among younger adults – especially, perhaps, social phobias (Grenier, et al, 2011).

Case study

Mike rang me at my clinic to talk to me about his wife, Lauren. Lauren was severely phobic about spiders and the phobia was increasingly impacting on her life. It used to be more manageable – she would just scream if she saw a spider and Mike would have to kill it or get rid of it. It wasn't really a big problem. Gradually, however, the phobia had become more severe. She began to avoid certain rooms in the house where she had seen spiders – particularly the downstairs toilet, and one of the children's rooms. She wouldn't go into these rooms at all. But, it was all still manageable.

Lately, however, the situation had got much worse. Mike thought it was after she had seen a really big spider in the park – there was quite a spate of spiders after some warm wet weather and everywhere was affected. Lauren began to avoid going to the park with the kids. She'd get panicky, start hyperventilating and become convinced that she was going to collapse or faint. The kids would get scared too and Lauren found the best thing was just to avoid parks.

Recently things had got even worse. She started avoiding the kitchen which was obviously a big problem because she needed to feed the kids. She coped by relying on the microwave more and more which she had moved to the morning room. Obviously Mike was very concerned and wasn't sure things could go on like this much longer.

However, when I asked Mike if Lauren acknowledged that she had a problem he said she seemed to be in denial. She refused to admit anything was wrong, and that having what she called a 'slight phobia' didn't constitute a major problem. She even claimed that Mike was the one with the problem as he was the one who seemed so bothered by it all!

I advised Mike that Lauren wasn't ready yet to tackle her phobia. We could all see that it was a problem but she was still in the denial stage. She couldn't be treated until she at least recognized that she had a problem. Mike was just going to have to be patient and wait. I did suggest that he bought her a self-help book and left it lying around – that might prompt her to recognize her problem.

Mike did this and three months later, Lauren herself rang me. She had read some of the case studies in the book and recognized some of what she was reading in herself. The book was useful but she felt that she needed more intensive input from a professional to help her overcome her phobia.

What causes phobias?

Many people with a phobia are desperate to know what has triggered it. Often, they will have a pretty good idea themselves, like Batya in the Underground case study, who clearly learned her fear from her mother (who herself developed the phobia after a traumatic incident – getting stuck on a Tube train). There are a number of reasons why people might develop a phobia and these are outlined below.

▶ Conditioning

It is possible to induce a phobia, especially in children, by simply pairing a harmless stimulus with one that naturally instils fear. For example, if we were to present a cuddly teddy bear to a small child while at the same time screaming at them, they would most likely become fearful of the teddy. That fear might *generalize* to other soft toys too. This is a conditioned (or learned) response and is maintained by the fact that we tend to avoid things that we are scared of – this means that we never learn to 'unlearn' the conditioned response. Thus a traumatic event, such as being bitten by a dog, can spark a phobia.

▶ Learning from other people

So-called vicarious learning means that we can acquire a phobia by copying someone else, like Batya in the case study did. Thus, phobias are often transmitted from parent to child. Studies have shown that parents who show their fear more often to their children have more fearful children than those who hide their fears (Coelho and Purkis, 2009). This happens because children (a) use the information given to them by parents to develop their own fear and (b) they learn to copy or model their parent's behaviours. In addition, (c) observing someone else's fear can also induce fear (Coelho and Purkis, 2009).

▶ 'Theory of Preparedness'

In 1971 a psychologist called Seligman suggested that some things or stimuli are 'evolutionarily predisposed' to evoke fear (Coelho and Purkis, 2009). This partly explains why some phobias are more common than others, such as spider phobia (one of the most common). Presumably, in our evolutionary past, our ancestors would have encountered deadly spiders so a healthy fear of them could save their lives. This, though, doesn't explain why not everyone is phobic of spiders. The Theory of Preparedness goes further then, by suggesting that some people are more biologically 'prepared' to have phobias than others. It is even possible that this 'preparedness' trait gave an evolutionary advantage in that more fearful people may have had better survival rates as they avoided more of the dangerous stimuli in life. Indeed, most specific phobias do involve situations that might have posed a threat in some way at some point in our evolutionary past.

Of course, this theory is not without its problems. It doesn't explain why spiders are common phobias when we are actually more likely to come across a mushroom that is lethal than a spider that is (Coelho and Purkis, 2009)!

▶ First Contact Theory

This theory is related to the above in that it builds on evolutionary principles. A lot of people don't suffer any traumatic episode that can account for their phobia, nor have they learnt it from their parents. These sufferers often report having 'always' been phobic since they were small children, without an obvious cause. The theory goes that it is a survival instinct to be afraid of something the first time we meet it (or contact it). This makes us wary until we know whether the new object is safe. This explains why children are often scared of new things or experiences, such as water, thunder, dogs etc. While most children overcome this fear, some get 'stuck' and remain fearful for life.

Why then, might some children get 'stuck' and remain fearful? Some psychologists suggest that children who are able to develop more control over their world, are more capable of dealing with scary situations and thus less likely to get 'stuck' on the things that they feared when they had their 'first contact' with them.

▶ Cultural factors

Some phobias are more common in some cultures than others. The most studied example of this is called *taijin kyofusho* which is thought to be a Japanese variant of social phobia based on excessive fear of harming or offending other people (Greenberg, Stravynski and Bilu, 2004). Similarly, a woman's unwillingness to leave the house might be regarded as severe agoraphobia in many cultures, but in some religious Muslim cultures, might be regarded as a virtue. Ultra-Orthodox Jewish men who are unwilling to interact with the opposite gender, or even engage in small talk with their own gender, might similarly be held in high esteem, while this might be regarded as evidence of a severe social phobia outside this environment (Greenberg, Stravynski and Bilu, 2004).

Key idea

Understanding why you have a phobia can be a helpful (though not essential) part of the treatment process.

What help is available for phobia sufferers?

Several chapters of this book will be devoted to self-help of phobic and related conditions, and these are based on *cognitive behavioural therapy* which is one of the techniques with the most proven efficacy rate. However, there are other options in terms of treatment and accessing treatment – some of which are more effective than others. It is worth mentioning what is available here, because many sufferers don't realize that there are various approaches out there – they might have tried a less effective approach, found it didn't work, then convince themselves that they are incurable. The fault may be with the approach, not the person using it!

▶ Cognitive behavioural therapy (CBT)

This is the treatment of choice for most psychologists and has a proven success record using scientific trials and studies. CBT uses both cognitive (involving thoughts) and behavioural (involving physical processes) techniques to tackle phobias and is the basis of most of the methods used in this book.

▶ Medication

Medication is not usually prescribed for treating phobias as CBT or other approaches are usually very successful. However, medication can be used to treat the symptoms of phobias (such as panic attacks – see Chapter 2) or to help sufferers who are extremely anxious a lot of the time (see Chapter 3 on anxiety). These medications can only be prescribed by a medical practitioner such as your family doctor or a psychiatrist. A psychologist or CBT trainer/counsellor, will not prescribe medication (although this might be changing in some US states), but may work with you using other approaches while you are also taking medication. Chapter 2 outlines more information about what medications are available, what they do, how they work and what their side-effects are.

▶ Hypnotherapy

Hypnosis is when a practitioner induces a mental state in the client or patient that makes them highly susceptible to suggestion. While most research on phobia treatments has concluded that cognitive behavioural therapy is the most effective treatment of choice, many practitioners claim great success with hypnosis.

▶ Alternative or complementary approaches

These approaches are generally unproven in terms of scientific studies and thus tend not to be adopted by psychologists (who are bound to use only proven techniques like CBT). However, therapists using alternative methods claim great success with techniques such as 'tapping' (tapping on the body's 'invisible energy pathways'), neuro-linguistic programming (NLP) and other approaches.

HOW TO OBTAIN PROFESSIONAL HELP FOR YOUR PHOBIA

There are generally two approaches to seeking help – the 'medical' or private route. The medical route usually involves referral to a clinical psychologist via your general practitioner or family doctor. Clinical psychologists generally work in hospital or clinical settings, and in the UK these treatments are available free on the NHS. However, many people are reluctant to go down this route because of long waiting lists, poor choice of appointment times or not wanting a note on their medical record.

The alternative then is private treatment where the client can self-refer. Obviously these treatments cost and the price can vary greatly. The quality of treatment can vary widely too, with little quality control over private practitioners. Some private health insurers cover the cost of psychological therapies but many do not.

	Advantages	Disadvantages
Medical route	Best chance of encountering effective treatments Free (in the UK)	Long waiting lists Will appear on your medical record Little choice of appointment time so may impact on work life etc. Therapist may not be able to accompany you out and about if required
Private route	More flexibility with appointment times Usually no waiting times for appointments Can have as many appointments as required More likely to get intensive therapy which NHS may not have time for (e.g. accompanying clients when facing phobia etc.) Usually comfortable and pleasant surroundings Can self-refer: no need to go through doctor Nothing on medical record	Cost involved Some may use unproven techniques

Key idea

Self-help books can be the first point of call for phobia sufferers but those who require more intensive or interactive help should either go through their family doctor or contact a private practitioner.

Focus points

❋ Phobias differ from normal fears in that they are excessive, severe, persistent and they limit the normal day to day life of the sufferer in some way.

❋ Symptoms of phobias are actually indicative of a normal, healthy stress response – it's just that these symptoms are displayed in inappropriate situations.

❋ Sufferers need to acknowledge that they have a problem before they can be helped.

❋ Many phobics can trace the origins of their phobia to some incident in their childhood or to parental influence – but not all phobias have an obvious cause. Knowing why you have the phobia is not relevant to treating it.

❋ There are numerous ways of treating phobias so if you have tried one approach with little success, don't give up!

2

Introduction to panic attacks

In this chapter you will learn:

- ▶ *What a panic attack is*
- ▶ *What causes panic attacks*
- ▶ *About the symptoms of panic attacks*
- ▶ *What help is available*

How do you feel?

1 Panic attacks are taking over my life — True/False

2 I live in fear of my next panic attack — True/False

3 I am afraid of what might happen if I don't escape when I have a panic attack — True/False

4 I avoid going places where I might have a panic attack — True/False

5 I would do anything to avoid a panic attack — True/False

If you have ticked 'True' for any of the above items, then this chapter is for you!

What are panic attacks?

According to the diagnostic guidelines set in the *Diagnostic and Statistical Manual* (known in the trade as DSM-IV, for the 4th edition of the manual) which is published by the American Psychiatric Association (1994), a panic attack is defined as:

> 'A discrete period in which there is the sudden onset of intense apprehension, fearfulness or terror often associated with feelings of impending doom.'

One of the key features of a panic attack is the quite sudden 'rush of fear' that peaks very quickly (Teng, et al, 2008). This fear is accompanied by a range of quite debilitating physical and emotional symptoms (see next section) and the whole experience is usually extremely frightening for the sufferer. The attack is often so frightening that the sufferer will go to great lengths to avoid another one.

Remember this

Panic attacks are terrifying! Unless you have actually experienced one, you cannot understand just how worrying panic attacks are for sufferers and why they will do anything to avoid a repeat occurrence.

When these attacks recur and are accompanied by the overwhelming fear of further attacks, they may lead to a condition known as 'panic disorder'.

Sometimes, the condition improves (perhaps with treatment or help of some kind) but may return at a later date.

WHO GETS PANIC ATTACKS?

It is thought that between 1 and 3.5 per cent of the population suffer from panic disorder (i.e. recurrent panic attacks) and they appear to be most common among adolescents and young adults (Teng, et al, 2008). If you reach your mid-forties without having had a panic attack, the chances are that you won't develop them.

Remember this

Adolescents and young adults (up to age about 35) are most commonly affected by panic attacks.

Symptoms of panic attacks

According to the DSM-IV guidelines, the intense fear characteristic of panic attacks must also be accompanied by at least four out of a list of symptoms for it to be classified as a panic attack (see diagnostic quiz below). Symptoms tend to fall into the following categories:

▶ **Heart-related symptoms:** such as palpitations, faster heart beat, pounding heart, chest pain etc.

▶ **Breathing-related:** difficulty catching breath, feeling breathless, fast breathing, shallow breathing

▶ **Muscle/skin/nerve symptoms:** trembling, shaking, jerking, spasms, numbness tingling, tremors, hot flushes, 'pins and needles', 'whooshing' noise in ears

▶ **Digestion-related symptoms:** feeling sick, difficulty swallowing

▶ **Emotional symptoms:** fear of going mad, feeling of being 'out of it' or outside one's own body, feeling of unreality, depression.

Diagnostic quiz of panic attack symptoms

When you have a panic attack, indicate how likely it is that you will experience each of the following symptoms:

	1 Very likely to occur	2 Quite likely to occur	3 Not very likely to occur	4 Never occurs
Palpitations, pounding heart or increased heart rate				
Sweating				
Trembling or shaking				
Shortness of breath				
Sensation of choking				
Chest pain or discomfort				
Nausea or stomach discomfort				
Dizziness, feeling unsteady, light-headed or faint				
Feeling of being 'out of it' or detached				
Fear of losing control				
Fear of dying				
Numbness or tingling feeling				
Having chills or hot flushes				
Fear of losing bladder or bowel control				

If you scored 1 or 2 for four or more of the above items, then it seems likely that you are indeed experiencing panic attacks.

One study suggests that the most common symptoms of panic attacks are 'heart pounding' which almost all sufferers claim to experience during a panic attack, closely followed by dizziness (Craske, et al, 2010). Numbness or tingling (sometimes known as paraesthesia) is experienced by around three-quarters of sufferers during a panic episode. Another study suggested that choking is the least commonly reported symptom – experienced only in around a third of sufferers (Craske, et al, 2010).

Remember this

Palpitations or a pounding heart is the most common symptom of a panic attack.

Are all panic attacks the same?

While most people suffering panic attacks (PAs) will experience similar symptoms, researchers over the years have suggested that not all panic attacks are the same. In fact, three different types of panic attack have been identified by many researchers and these will be described in the following sections.

Mythbuster

Not all panic attacks are the same. People can have different symptoms and some people can even experience them in their sleep.

RESPIRATORY TYPE

The respiratory PA is characterized by a number of common symptoms; to find out if your PAs are of the respiratory type, indicate whether you have experienced any of the following during your most *recent* PA:

Feeling of choking	Yes/No
Shortness of breath	Yes/No
Chest pain/discomfort	Yes/No
Numbness/tingling sensations	Yes/No
Fear of dying from symptoms	Yes/No

If, during your last PA, you experienced four out of the above five symptoms, then yours might be classed as a respiratory type of PA.

Some studies have shown that this type of PA is more likely to be associated with a family history of PAs (i.e. another member of your family may also have or have had this type of PA). This type of PA is also thought to begin at an earlier age than other types and to last longer (Kircanski, et al, 2009).

NOCTURNAL TYPE

This type of PA is characterized by waking up in a state of panic – in other words, it has the usual symptoms of panic, but it comes on apparently unexpectedly while the sufferer is asleep. Sufferers usually have daytime PAs too (often of the respiratory type), though some may only have them at night. Research suggests that there is no physical cause for the attacks – i.e. there is no problem with the heart or other sleep disorders that might account for the attack.

One study suggested that around 58 per cent of people with daytime PAs have experienced at least one nocturnal PA too and around a third of PA sufferers regularly have night-time attacks (Kircanski, et al, 2009). Once a sufferer has a nocturnal attack, they often find it hard to get back to sleep and are fearful of having another attack – this can lead to severe sleep difficulties as they start to fear and avoid going to sleep (see Chapter 5 for more on this).

These sleep problems can lead to daytime difficulties with normal functioning and thus lead to other problems associated with severe sleep disturbances (such as depression: see Chapter 10).

VESTIBULAR TYPE

Dizziness is the main characteristic of this type of PA and this feeling of dizziness may occur both during the PA and between panic attacks. Dizziness during PAs is a fairly common feature, but vestibular types are more likely to report this as being one of their most severe symptoms; they are also more likely to complain of feeling dizzy more generally, even when not in an acute PA episode. Sufferers of vestibular type PA may be more likely to experience agoraphobia and other complex phobias (see Chapter 6) than other PA types.

Why do panic attacks occur?

Cognitions, or thoughts, play a central role in panic attack disorder. The physical symptoms of PAs on their own, would not be enough to lead to recurrent attacks. After all, we all experience most of the physical symptoms of PAs every time we do something energetic such as run for the bus, but we don't usually feel panicky at these times. This is because we can attribute the symptoms to something – we can ascribe the increased heart rate, shortness of breath etc, to the fact that we have run for the bus. We thus, do not feel afraid or panicky about our pounding heart or sweaty face. We don't assume that a heart attack is imminent or that we are going crazy. We have a logical and reasonable explanation for the symptoms.

Mythbuster

The symptoms of a panic attack are not what cause the attack – it is how we interpret these symptoms that causes the anxiety.

However, when the same symptoms appear 'out of the blue' and we can't easily ascribe a reason for their appearance, some people become extremely fearful of them. It is the fear of these symptoms that leads to further attacks and to the avoidance behaviour so typical of the PA sufferer. This is why, in Chapter 5, we will see that the first line of treatment is education about the causes of symptoms so that they can be explained – making them less open to fear and misinterpretation.

The fears about the symptoms are often based on 'catastrophic misinterpretations' of the physical and psychological symptoms associated with PAs (Raffa, White and Barlow, 2004). The theory behind this is that lots of people may experience the physical symptoms of 'panic attack' for a range of reasons – but it is only by misinterpreting these symptoms in a catastrophic way that the panic attack disorder is born.

In other words, the symptoms may be relatively harmless on their own, but if the sufferer believes that they are likely to indicate an imminent heart attack, or that they are about to collapse or even die, they panic; it is these catastrophic interpretations of their symptoms that gives rise to the feeling of panic – leading to intense fear of having further attacks.

Interestingly, it is thought that PA sufferers are more likely to misinterpret their harmless physical symptoms in a catastrophic way than non-PA sufferers. In other words, lots of people may occasionally experience the physical, unexpected symptoms of panic attacks – but some people are both more sensitive to these physical sensations and more likely to misinterpret them as something dangerous (e.g. as precursors to a heart attack). This is the so-called Cognitive Model of Panic Disorder or Catastrophic Cognitions Theory first proposed by Clark in 1986 (Austin and Richards, 2006). More on this later in the chapter.

Remember this

Panic attack sufferers are likely to misinterpret their physical symptoms as something dangerous which makes them even more fearful and leads to greater intensity of the symptoms.

The fear, then, that results from panickers misattributing harmless reactions to dangerous causes, in turn leads to an increase in *sympathetic arousal* in the body. Sympathetic arousal is the response our body makes to fearful or stressful situations – our heart beats faster, our blood pressure rises etc.; all the reactions associated with 'fight or flight' response that was discussed in Chapter 1 (and will be outlined further in Chapter 3). Thus, our fear of the bodily symptoms leads to even more physical symptoms – which leads to even more fear as we become even more convinced that a terrible catastrophe is about to occur (e.g. a heart attack). This feedback loop leads to an escalation of both fear and symptoms of panic (see Figure 2.1).

Key idea

Understanding the physiology of how panic attacks happen is an important first step to treating them.

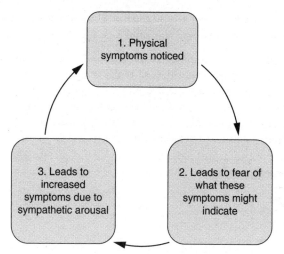

Figure 2.1 Feedback loop leading to an escalation of both fear and symptoms of panic

Panic attacks and other conditions

Panic attacks often occur alongside other conditions (Figure 2.2). These include:

▷ **General anxiety disorder.** GAD (see Chapter 3) is often a precursor to panic attacks in that high states of anxiety can give rise to the symptoms of a panic attack. PA sufferers often have quite high levels of generalized anxiety even when not in their feared situation or when actually experiencing a panic attack.

▷ **Specific/simple phobias.** Panic attacks are often experienced when phobic people face the object of their fear. Panic attacks are probably one of the most common symptoms of a true phobia.

▷ **Complex phobias.** Panic attacks can lead to the development of social phobia or agoraphobia (see Chapter 6) because sufferers learn to avoid situations that they fear will lead them to panic. Panic attacks tend to happen more in public places when there is the fear of social sanction (e.g. embarrassment of shaking or fainting etc.) or fear of being unable to access medical care (if fears are of having a heart attack) or accessing a toilet (if fears involve worries of losing bowel/bladder control). These fears can lead to sufferers avoiding public places and thus lead to these complex phobias (see Chapter 6 for more).

▶ **Depression.** Panic attacks can have such a debilitating effect on people that they can really take over. Sufferers can find their world gets smaller as they are unable to lead a normal life or even, in extreme cases, leave the house. Not surprisingly, this can lead to severe depression which will be discussed in more detail in Chapter 10.

Remember this
Panic attacks, if left untreated, can lead to the development of other conditions too.

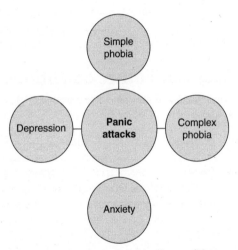

Figure 2.2 Relationship of panic attacks with other conditions

Case study
Zelda came to my clinic because of what she described as her 'nerves'. She was having regular panic attacks and these had got so bad that she was becoming more and more limited in what she could do. At the first session it transpired that Zelda had always been what she described as a 'nervous' type. She was always anxious, a worrier. She worried about everything and spent a lot of time going over in her mind all the things

that could go wrong. She found it hard to make decisions because she was so worried about making the wrong one. She liked her life to be predictable and as safe as possible.

However, recently she had started to get severe attacks of anxiety which matched the symptoms of panic attacks. The first one happened at a social gathering – a small dinner party with friends. She was feeling quite anxious about it because she had never thought that she was very good at social events – she always felt very self-conscious and never knew what to say or how to behave. She always felt that everyone was looking at her and thinking she was boring or dull or even stupid. As a result, at the dinner, she started to feel a bit flustered and suddenly felt that she couldn't breathe. She felt hot and sweaty and her heart was pounding. She felt dizzy and felt sure she was going to faint or have a heart attack. Her friends noticed and asked if she was OK and she mumbled that she felt a bit unwell and rushed out. She felt better once she got some fresh air, but felt so embarrassed that she made her excuses – something about coming down with a cold – and left.

The next day she went to see her doctor who examined her and declared her fit and well. He said it was 'just' a panic attack and nothing to worry about. Zelda was relieved that it wasn't anything serious but felt even more embarrassed about it when her friends rang to see if she was OK. She didn't want to admit that it was a panic attack so pretended to be flu-ish.

The next time she saw her friends, she was terrified of it happening again. She could hardly claim to be ill a second time so she knew that she mustn't have another attack. This time they were meeting up for coffee and they had just sat down when she started to feel hot again and felt sure another attack was on its way. She quickly went to the toilets to calm down but when she went back she realized that this 'escape route' could only be used once or her friends would think her odd. She was terrified of the panic coming back – what could she do then? She tried to distract herself but soon she began to feel hot and breathless again. She knew that if she didn't get out of there she would have a full-blown attack and maybe faint or even wet herself. She jumped up and made some excuse about suddenly remembering she was late for an appointment and rushed off.

After that, she never met up with her friends again in case the panic came back. She made excuses and soon they stopped inviting her. But, her panic attacks didn't stop. She began to worry about getting them in other places too – such as in meetings at work. In fact, anywhere that it would be difficult to escape from without people thinking she was odd. She began to avoid situations like this as much as possible, which was obviously affecting her work life too. She turned down projects that would involve meeting new people.

She stopped going out socially and her work was suffering. She began to feel depressed as her world got smaller. She didn't feel she could tell anyone about her problems and lived in fear of the next panic attack. Before long, she was seeing her doctor for depression and he prescribed anti-depressants and she was signed off work with a sick note. Not going to work made her feel even more depressed and her situation was getting desperate.

Quiz: what do you fear?
Everyone who has panic attacks fears some major consequence of their attack, i.e. that something terrible will happen to them. When you have a PA, how afraid are you that the following will happen:

	1 Very afraid	2 Afraid	3 Sometimes afraid	4 Never afraid
That I will vomit				
That I will faint				
That I will lose control of my bladder or bowels (that I will wet or soil myself)				
That I will die				
That other people will notice me shaking				

You might be relieved to know that the chances of these things actually happening are very small. For example, if you have never actually fainted (during a panic attack), but fear that you will, then research would suggest that you are not likely to actually faint. (In fact, it is quite difficult to faint during a panic attack because panic attacks are associated with an increase in blood pressure, whereas faints are usually associated with a decrease in blood pressure.)

Key idea

Knowing that you are unlikely to suffer catastrophic consequences from a panic attack can help you not to fear them as much.

Most of the above fears are to do with social consequences of the panic attack – people worry they will have symptoms that other people will notice and will embarrass themselves. It is this fear that feeds the panic, as explained above. There is also an element of the fear being that they are not in a place of 'safety' where medical help/toilets etc. are available. Coping with these fears will be discussed in later chapters.

Mythbuster

Many sufferers feel that they will faint when they have a panic attack but in reality this is quite unlikely due to the raised blood pressure that usually accompanies panic attacks.

Why do some people get panic attacks and others don't?

If everyone occasionally experiences symptoms of a PA (as explained earlier), but only some go on to develop the disorder, what is it that makes PA sufferers different? Why, for example, are they more likely to interpret their symptoms as catastrophic? One theory is that some people might be more genetically prone to suffer from PAs than others. These people are likely to be more sensitive to stress in general and to notice physical symptoms more readily. Their genetic vulnerability makes them more likely to consider benign symptoms as being potentially dangerous and to see general life stressors as being more threatening than they really are.

This theory holds that people who are susceptible to PAs are those high on the personality trait of 'anxiety sensitivity'. A key feature here is the 'notion of excessive reaction to somatic sensations' (Austin and Richards, 2006). In other worse, it is the fear of the symptoms that drives the panic attacks and some people are just more prone to catastrophizing their fear than others. Indeed, studies show that when presented with the same harmless bodily sensations (which can be manipulated by researchers), PA-prone people will interpret these as signs of impending harm or catastrophe far more than less PA-prone individuals do. In fact, this tendency (to misinterpret harmless symptoms as something catastrophic) might well precede the onset of panic attack disorder.

Another theory to explain why some people develop PAs is the so-called 'hyperventilation theory' (Roth, Wilhelm and Pettit, 2005). The suggestion here is that it is the decreased level of arterial pCO_2 (partial pressure of carbon dioxide) that is associated with hyperventilation which leads to feelings of extreme anxiety. Hyperventilation, sometimes called over-breathing, is when you breathe very fast and deep breaths; this affects the carbon dioxide levels in your body which can lead to a range of symptoms (similar to symptoms of a PA) including severe anxiety – i.e. breathing too quickly, which we do when we are anxious, can cause panic. However, as PAs can also cause hyperventilation, it is difficult to really be sure about which comes first. Certainly breathing exercises are an important factor in controlling PAs as we will see in Chapter 5.

Do your panic attacks need treating?

Single episodes of panic should not be a cause for concern. However, single episodes can sometimes be so dreadful that sufferers will do anything to avoid a repeat occurrence. This often starts an avoidance–fear cycle that can severely limit the life of the sufferer. An example of such an avoidance–fear cycle is shown in Figure 2.3. The diagram shows how a random, one-off Panic Attack (PA) can end up as PA disorder.

The sufferer may experience a 'random' attack that seems to appear out of the blue. In actual fact, there may be underlying reasons for the attack to occur – pre-conditions that make the attack happen at that time. For example, the sufferer may have been feeling especially stressed or anxious, may have been

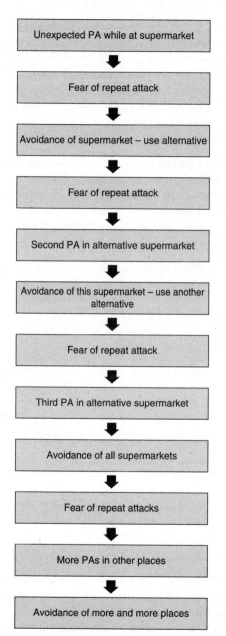

Figure 2.3 Avoidance–fear cycle of panic attack

rushing around, may be hot, thirsty, hungry etc. All of these can lead to symptoms that can cause alarm in those predisposed to the sort of catastrophic misinterpretation described above; the sufferer notices their increased heart rate etc., and is convinced that these symptoms are signs of an impending heart attack. This fear leads to a rapid increase in anxiety and this leads to further symptoms which are interpreted as more evidence of impending catastrophe.

The full-blown panic attack is so terrifying that the sufferer escapes in order to feel safe again. They tend to feel better once they are in a 'safer' place – for example, away from crowds who might witness their attack. In order to avoid a repeat performance, they avoid the place that the attack happened in (e.g. the supermarket) and use an alternative.

The problem is that they now start to get anxious in the alternative supermarket. They worry that the PA might recur. This worry leads to more sympathetic arousal (see Figure 2.1) and more symptoms of anxiety – which can lead to a second panic attack. Again, the sufferer escapes – and starts to avoid the second supermarket.

This cycle continues until the sufferer is experiencing attacks in a wide range of places – all of which are added to the list of 'places to avoid'. It can even get to the stage when sufferers can barely leave their house for fear of another PA. It is usually at this stage that a sufferer will seek professional help.

Key idea

If you are avoiding places that you would normally go to because of fear of having a panic attack then your panic attacks need sorting!

As with phobias, there are generally three stages to seeking help for panic attacks:

▶ **Stage 1**

Acknowledgement that there is a problem. Unless someone realizes that they have a problem, they won't seek help and many people remain in denial for quite a long time before accepting that their problem is serious enough to need help.

Why, then, do many people refuse to acknowledge that their panic attacks are a problem? In my experience, there are a range of reasons:

▶ People are ashamed or embarrassed to think that they might have a 'mental health' problem.

▶ They feel that they should be able to sort this out themselves.

▶ They get so used to adapting their life around their problem (e.g. avoiding the places where they get PAs) that they don't realize they are even doing so.

This denial can go on for some time and, quite often, it is other people close to the sufferer who acknowledge the problem first and try to encourage them to seek help.

▶ Stage 2

Seeking self-help. Here the sufferer realizes that they have a problem and that they need to get some outside input. They are not yet ready to seek professional help for a number of reasons:

▶ They don't think their problem is so bad that it needs professional help.

▶ They are embarrassed or ashamed to go to a 'mental health professional'.

▶ They are worried that seeing a therapist will go on their medical record and affect employment prospects etc.

▶ They haven't got time to go to clinic appointments.

▶ Their panic attacks are still manageable in that they are not restricting their life too much.

Self-help is available in many forms, including books like this, internet advice etc.

▶ Stage 3

This is where professional help is sought either via NHS referral from the family doctor or with private therapists or trainers.

Often a sufferer will have tried the self-help route and either not chosen a good source of self-help for them, or else their problem is so severe that they really need professional input.

If you are reading this book then you are probably in Stage 2 at least, but in case you still want to know whether your panic attacks needs treating, answer the questions in the quiz below.

Quiz: Do your panic attacks need treating?

	1 Never	2 Sometimes	3 Often	4 Very often
Do your panic attacks stop you doing things you want to do?				
Do they stop you leading a normal life (e.g. going shopping)?				
Do your panic attacks affect your work or your ability to work?				
Do your panic attacks affect your social life?				
Are you limited or restricted in where you go because of your panic attacks (or fear of panic attacks)?				
Do your panic attacks (or fear of them) affect your quality of life?				

If you score more than 2 on at least three items, then your panic attacks do need sorting!

Case study

Jack was a university student in his first year of study. One day in his first term, he rushed to an early morning lecture. He had been up partying till late the night before, overslept, didn't have time for breakfast and got to the lecture hall late. He was a bit self-conscious as he slunk in and took his place but, about ten minutes later he suddenly had a panic attack. He was shaking, felt that he would choke, couldn't swallow, his heart was pounding and he felt sure something terrible was going to happen to him. He had never experienced anything like this before. He was terrified. He didn't want to get up and leave because he had already drawn attention to himself by arriving late, but he felt he had no choice. He whispered to his friend that 'something is happening to me' and he staggered out with his friend following.

His friend took him straight to a walk-in clinic and they wired up his heart and declared him fine. He was very relieved and put it all down to the rushing around, not eating, being hung-over etc.

However, the next time he was in a lecture, he began to worry that if he had another panic attack, he wouldn't easily be able to escape. He had already drawn attention to himself the first time – to do so again would be too embarrassing. He began frantically looking around to see where the exits were and tried to calm down. He managed to resist the temptation to leave but by the lecture break, he was sweating profusely and just couldn't take anymore. He left and didn't go back.

From then on, he tried to sit close to the exits in lectures but it didn't make any difference. He kept panicking and having to leave. He didn't tell anyone about his problem as he felt it wasn't cool for such a young lad to get this sort of thing. He was missing a lot of lecture material because he was leaving halfway through or was too panicky to concentrate when he was there. He started to struggle with his work and got even more stressed, and soon stopped going to lectures altogether. He still wouldn't admit he had a problem and just told his mates that the lectures were boring.

After two months he quit his course – it was inevitable as he was missing so much. But he wouldn't tell anyone the real reason – he told his family that 'university wasn't for me'. It took him a further 18 months before he acknowledged the problem – and that was only because he started to get panic attacks all the time – and sought professional help.

What help is available for panic attack sufferers?

Several chapters of this book will be devoted to self-help of panic and related conditions, and these are based on *cognitive behavioural therapy* which is one of the techniques with the most proven efficacy rate. However, there are other options in terms of treatment and accessing treatment – some of which are more effective than others. It is worth mentioning what is available here, because many sufferers don't realize that there are various approaches out there – they might have tried a less effective approach, found it didn't work, then convinced themselves that they were incurable. The fault may be with the approach, not the person using it!

▶ Cognitive behavioural therapy (CBT)

This is the treatment of choice for most psychologists and has a proven success record in scientific trials and studies. CBT uses both cognitive (involving thoughts) and behavioural (involving physical processes) techniques to tackle phobias and is the basis of most of the methods used in this book.

▶ Medication

Medication can be used to treat panic attacks or to help sufferers who are extremely anxious a lot of the time (see Chapter 3 on anxiety). Such medication can only be prescribed by a medical practitioner such as your family doctor or a psychiatrist. A psychologist or CBT trainer/counsellor will not prescribe medication (although this might be changing in some US states), but may work with you using other approaches while you are also taking medication.

There are three main types of medication used for treating the severe anxiety associated with panic attacks. These include anti-depressants, tranquillizers and beta-blockers (http://www.nhs.uk/Conditions/Phobias/Pages/Treatment.aspx).

Anti-depressants prescribed to help reduce anxiety include:

- ▶ Paroxetine (known as Seroxat), a selective serotonin reuptake inhibitor (SSRI), which is licensed to treat social phobia (see Chapter 6);

- ▶ Citalopram (Cipramil) and E (Cipralex), which are licensed for the treatment of panic disorders;

- ▶ Venlafaxine (Efexor), which is licensed for generalized anxiety disorder (GAD) (see Chapter 3);

- ▶ Clomipramine (Anafranil) which is a type of tricyclic anti-depressant (TCA) licensed to treat phobias;

- ▶ Moclobemide (Manerix) which is a type of anti-depressant from the monoamine oxidase inhibitor (MAOI) group of anti-depressants sometimes prescribed to treat social phobia.

It is important to note (and your doctor should tell you) that these medications may have side-effects such as nausea, sleep problems, blurred vision, palpitations and headaches. Different medications can have different side-effects so it is important to be aware of these if you decide to take them. They can even make anxiety worse before it gets better. Anti-depressants can also cause withdrawal symptoms so don't stop taking them suddenly.

Tranquillizers or benzodiazepines are sometimes used to treat severe anxiety, but are usually only prescribed in the lowest possible dose for the shortest possible time (usually around four weeks). This is because they are associated with withdrawal and addiction problems. Benzodiazepines that are often used include:

▶ diazepam (Valium);

▶ alprazolam (Xanax);

▶ chlordiazepoxide;

▶ lorazepam (Ativan);

▶ oxazepam.

Like anti-depressants, these drugs can also cause side-effects.

Beta-blockers are drugs used to treat cardiovascular conditions, such as heart problems and high blood pressure (hypertension) but are also sometimes prescribed to help reduce the symptoms of anxiety, such as palpitations (irregular heartbeat). Beta-blockers slow down your heart rate and decrease your blood pressure. Propranolol (Inderal) is a beta-blocker that is commonly used to treat anxiety.

▶ Hypnotherapy

During hypnosis the practitioner induces a mental state in the client or patient that makes them highly susceptible to suggestion. While most research on panic treatments has concluded that cognitive behavioural therapy is the most effective treatment of choice, many practitioners claim great success with hypnosis.

▶ Alternative or complementary approaches

These approaches are generally unproven in terms of scientific studies (although alternative practitioners will no doubt disagree with this statement) and thus tend not to be adopted by psychologists (who are bound to use only proven techniques like CBT). However, therapists using alternative methods claim great success with techniques such as 'tapping' (tapping on the body's 'invisible energy pathways'), neuro-linguistic programming (NLP) and other approaches.

HOW TO OBTAIN HELP FOR YOUR PANIC ATTACKS

As for phobias, there are generally two approaches to seeking help – the 'medical' and the private route. The medical route usually involves referral to a clinical psychologist via your general practitioner or family doctor. Clinical psychologists generally work in hospital or clinical settings and in the UK these treatments are available free on the NHS. However, many people are reluctant to go down this route because of long waiting lists, poor choice of appointment times or not wanting it on their medical record.

The alternative then is private treatment where the client can self-refer. Obviously these treatments cost and the price can vary greatly. The quality of treatment can vary widely too, with little quality control over private practitioners.

See Chapter 1 for more on the advantages and disadvantages of using the medical vs the private route for treatment for your panic attacks (the advantages and disadvantages are the same as for seeking help with phobias).

Focus points

* Panic attacks are a normal 'fight or flight' stress reaction that happens at inappropriate times.
* Most sufferers fear that something terrible will happen to them but these fears are usually groundless.
* A first panic attack may appear to come 'out of the blue' but the fear of having a panic attack is the main cause of further attacks.
* Trying to avoid panic attacks sets up a cycle whereby sufferers can end up avoiding more and more situations in case they lead to panic.
* Panic attacks are often associated with other conditions, but CBT and other therapies are very effective at treating them.

3

Anxiety

In this chapter you will learn:

▶ *What anxiety is*
▶ *About generalized anxiety disorder (GAD)*
▶ *How general anxiety levels contribute to other disorders*
▶ *About treatment options for anxiety*
▶ *How to reduce your anxiety levels*

How do you feel?

1 Do you feel anxious most of the time?   Yes/No

2 Do you worry a lot?   Yes/No

3 Do you tend to always imagine the worst that could happen? Yes/No

4 Do you find it difficult to make decisions in case you choose the
   wrong option?   Yes/No

5 Do you find it difficult to relax?   Yes/No

If you answer 'yes' to more than two of these questions, then it
is worth reading this chapter. You might have generalized anxiety
disorder or you might just have high levels of anxiety. Either way, they
could be contributing to your panic attacks or phobias.

What is anxiety?

Anxiety is a stress response that is normal in certain,
threatening situations. It is normal and even helpful to get
anxious at times; for example, when faced with someone who
is aggressive towards you, or when approaching an important
examination. Without anxiety, we wouldn't be motivated to do
something about the threatening situation, such as run away,
or study hard. Anxiety has special evolutionary value in that it
would have helped our ancestors cope with anxiety-provoking
situations (like an advancing predator, or food shortage). This
is because anxiety, like stress and other powerful emotions, can
have a profound effect on the body. As our anxiety rises, the
hypothalamus in the brain stimulates the *pituitary gland* at the
base of the skull to release a range of hormones that affect every
part of our body in one way or another. These hormones are
similar to those released when we are stressed.

The main hormones are *adrenaline* and *cortisol*. Both these
hormones exert their influence through the *cardiovascular
system* (the system involving the heart) as well as other systems.

Adrenaline causes the heart to beat faster and blood pressure to
rise; this allows oxygen-rich blood to flow more quickly to the
areas of the body that are responsible for reacting to the source

of anxiety. These areas are those that need extra energy – for example, the arms (to fight) or the legs (to flee) and the brain (to think quickly).

When we are responding to a threat that causes us to get anxious, an immediate reaction is required so, while blood rushes to the limbs and brain, it is diverted from less important areas of the body like the stomach or skin – now is not the time for the body to be worrying about digestion or maintaining healthy skin. Instead all resources are diverted to concentrating on dealing with the immediate problem. It is just like a workplace coping with a crisis; all non-essential functions would stop while the employees dealt with the immediate emergency.

All this anticipated extra activity requires extra energy and the other important hormone, cortisol, is responsible for this bit of the anxiety reaction. The release of cortisol in the blood causes the liver to convert its emergency stores of energy (in the form of glycogen) into the more readily usable form of glucose. This extra glucose provides the surge of energy needed to beat the source of the anxiety.

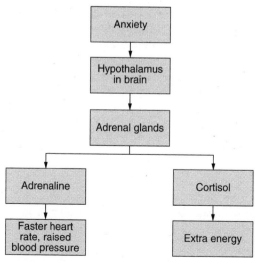

Figure 3.1 Anxiety response

The net effect of all this activity is a rapid heartbeat, breathlessness (as the lungs struggle to take in more oxygen), raised blood pressure (hypertension) and a raised body temperature (due to using more energy). All this made our anxious ancestors ideally placed to deal with the sources of their anxiety by either fighting their opponent or running away (this is the fight or flight response referred to in earlier chapters).

Remember this

Anxiety causes physical reactions in our bodies because it was designed to help us fight or flee.

Nowadays, however, these responses are less useful. Rarely do we have the chance to respond to things that make us anxious in the way that our bodily reactions are designed. So, instead of us making use of the extra energy and resources our bodies have provided us with, we are left with all this excessive anxiety.

How much anxiety is excessive?

We all know what it is to feel anxious but some people feel excessively anxious a lot of the time. Sometimes, this is referred to as having generalized anxiety disorder (GAD). Everyone feels anxious at times, but people with this condition feel tense and stressed most days and for most of the day. The anxiety can take over their lives and can lead to depression, as well as being the precursor for panic attacks and phobias. Anxiety is thought to be abnormal if:

▶ It is excessive or out of proportion to the source of the anxiety (e.g. sufferers might worry about the same things as everyone else like money etc. but take it to a much higher level).

▶ It persists when whatever has caused the anxious response has gone.

▶ It appears for no apparent reason when there is no specific situation that is causing anxiety (for example, over-reacting to a simple event such as someone not responding to a text – imagining something terrible has happened to them).

▶ It is almost constant.

▶ It is debilitating i.e. it affects and interferes with normal daily life.

People with GAD don't just feel anxious about the things that most people worry about (such as exams or results), but tend to feel generally anxious without there necessarily being a specific event or situation causing the anxiety. This differs then from phobias where there is a specific situation triggering the anxiety. GAD is less intense than a panic attack but persists for longer and can generally affect the whole quality of life for the sufferer.

Key idea

According to the DSM-IV, the criteria for diagnosing GAD are:

✳ Excessive anxiety and worry (apprehensive expectation), occurring more days than not for at least six months, about a number of events or activities (such as work or school performance).
✳ The person finds it difficult to control the worry.
✳ The anxiety and worry are associated with three (or more) of the following six symptoms (with at least some symptoms present for more-days-than-not for the past six months):
  ▷ restlessness or feeling keyed up or on edge
  ▷ being easily fatigued
  ▷ difficulty concentrating or mind going blank
  ▷ irritability
  ▷ muscle tension
  ▷ sleep disturbance (difficulty falling or staying asleep, or restless, unsatisfying sleep)
✳ The focus of the anxiety and worry is not confined to features of other disorders (such as social phobia, OCD, PTSD etc.)
✳ The anxiety, worry, or physical symptoms cause clinically significant distress or impairment in social, occupational, or other important areas of functioning. The disturbance is not due to the direct physiological effects of a substance (e.g. a drug of abuse, a medication) or a general medical condition (e.g., hyperthyroidism), and does not occur exclusively during a mood disorder, psychotic disorder, or a pervasive developmental disorder.

Remember this

Anxiety is excessive if it lasts a long time, seems out of proportion to its source and doesn't just have one cause (or persists once that cause has gone).

Are you excessively anxious?
How much do you agree with the following statements?

	1 Strongly disagree	2 Disagree	3 Agree	4 Strongly agree
I worry about things most of the day.				
I go over and over things in my mind.				
I can't stop worrying.				
I have so many worries.				
I can't help thinking that bad things are going to happen.				
I find it hard to concentrate because I am so preoccupied with my worries.				
People tell me I worry too much.				
I often feel tense.				
I often feel tearful.				
I find it hard to remember the last time I felt relaxed.				
I feel that my worrying protects me in some way: i.e. by worrying, the feared outcome is less likely to happen.				

If you scored 3s or 4s to more than five items, then you may have GAD.

WHO GETS GAD?

It is thought that GAD affects about 1 in 20 adults in the UK. Slightly more women are affected than men, and the condition is most common in people in their 20s.

▶ Symptoms of GAD

GAD can cause both psychological and physical symptoms. Psychological symptoms include:

- feeling restless;

- having a constant sense of dread or of impending doom;

- feeling constantly 'on edge';

- having problems concentrating on matters other than the worries;

- being easily distracted by worries or concerns;

- inability to work effectively;

- feeling depressed or worthless.

The physical symptoms of GAD can be similar to those experienced during panic attacks. Remember that for GAD sufferers, these symptoms occur much of the time, whereas with panic attacks, the symptoms come on suddenly and fade when the sufferer feels 'safe' again. With GAD, the sufferer never really feels 'safe' so the symptoms linger. Physical symptoms include:

- dizziness;

- drowsiness and tiredness;

- irregular heartbeat (palpitations);

- muscle aches and tension;

- dry mouth;

- excessive sweating;

- shortness of breath;

- stomach ache;

- nausea;

- diarrhoea;

- headache;

- irregular periods;

- difficulty falling or staying asleep (insomnia).

WHY DO SOME PEOPLE GET EXCESSIVELY ANXIOUS?

As mentioned earlier, there are often good evolutionary reasons for people to get anxious; anxiety may well have been necessary for our survival. However, this doesn't explain why some people suffer excessive anxiety and others seem to be able to take life's ups and downs in their stride. There are three possible theories to explain why some people suffer from GAD:

▶ Life events theory

People often develop anxiety following a series of stressful life events such as moving house, divorce, bereavement, redundancy etc. If a few stressful life events happen close together, it is perhaps not surprising that sufferers can become very tense and anxious; they might have been able to bounce back from one event, but two or more can use up their coping resources.

Life events can have another impact too: people can learn to be anxious based on their life experiences. For example, if they have had a health scare in the past, or a close friend has, they may become excessively anxious when reading about health issues.

▶ Thinking styles theory

Some people may have a thinking style that lends itself to experiencing greater anxiety. For example, anxious people have a tendency to expect that the worst possible scenario will always occur and that they must constantly be on their guard in case something bad happens. Anxious people often think that by imagining the worst-case scenario, they are protecting themselves in some way from that event happening, either because they will be better prepared, or because they superstitiously believe that worrying will prevent it actually happening; if they let their guard down, the terrible scenario might be 'allowed' to occur. CBT is particularly effective in dealing with these patterns of thinking (see later sections in this chapter).

▶ Genetic make-up

This theory holds that there is a genetic link in feeling excessively anxious so that if a close family member suffers from an anxiety disorder, then you might too.

Remember this

Your genetic make-up can be responsible for your problems with anxiety.

Case study

Ruth has always considered herself to be an anxious person. She would always worry about what 'might happen'. This has always made her very cautious – which she thinks is a good thing. She never takes risks because she worries too much about things going wrong. Her mum was exactly the same and Ruth grew up in a household where she was very protected and cosseted.

In fact, she grew up to be quite fearful of even the slightest risk and it had got to the point where Ruth found herself worrying so much about what could happen that she was living an ever-increasingly sheltered life. For example, she was afraid to go on holiday abroad – the risks just seemed too great. There's the flying – not just the terrifying risk of the plane crashing, but the whole experience – what if her cases were to go missing? What if she were to miss the flight? What if she were to get ill abroad or have an accident? It was all too daunting, with too many uncontrollable factors.

Ruth would only holiday in places she felt were very low-risk and safe. In fact, this meant that she went to the same hotel in the Lake District every year. She knew what to expect and felt very safe. She enjoyed it – but her husband was fed up and wanted to travel further afield. This is why Ruth came to the clinic – her husband had told her that it wasn't just the holidays, but the impact that her worrying was having on their whole lives. Ruth would rarely eat out as she didn't trust the food safety of many places. She rarely socialized with friends because she was worried that they would look down on her or think badly on her. Then there were the kids.

Ruth had two children aged six and nine. Her worries about the kids had always been manageable, but now they were starting to resent her control – she wouldn't let them do anything she considered to be 'risky'. This included paddling in the sea, having swimming lessons, going on school trips, or going on sleepovers. She was just too worried about everything and her anxieties were making her life miserable – and her family's lives.

High levels of generalized anxiety can be precursors to other
anxiety conditions, such as phobias, panic attacks and obsessive-
compulsive disorder. This is because anxious individuals tend to
be more threat-sensitive and aware of what can go wrong – they
are more fearful in general. This can make them vulnerable to
phobias. Their high levels of anxiety can also lead to physical
symptoms which can be misinterpreted in catastrophic ways –
leading to panic attacks. Anxious thoughts about health and
infection can to suffers become obsessive about hygiene and
hand-washing (obsessive–compulsive disorder – see Chapter 9).

Thus, lowering general levels of anxiety is the first step to
treating other anxiety-related conditions.

What are the treatment options?

▶ **Medication**

Before we go on to outline the self-help options it is useful
to point out that many medical practitioners will prescribe
medication to help with extreme anxiety. Drugs can be useful
when used alongside other approaches and some of the more
common drugs prescribed include:

Anti-depressants. While these are commonly used to treat
depression, they can also help reduce the symptoms of anxiety
even if you are not depressed. Research trials suggest that
anti-depressants can ease symptoms in over half of people
with GAD. They work by interfering with brain chemicals
(neurotransmitters) such as serotonin, the lack of which may
be involved in causing anxiety symptoms. They do take around
a month to take effect. Sometimes medication can make the
anxiety get worse before it gets better.

There are several types of anti-depressants, though *selective
serotonin reuptake inhibitor (SSRI)* anti-depressants are
the ones most commonly used for anxiety disorders. Two
commonly used SSRIs to treat GAD are escitalopram and
paroxetine. Other anti-depressants that have been found to help
include venlafaxine and duloxetine.

Buspirone. This medicine is another option to treat GAD. It is an anti-anxiety drug, but different from the benzodiazepines (discussed below). It is not clear how it works, but it is known to affect serotonin, a brain chemical which may be involved in causing anxiety symptoms.

Benzodiazepines, such as diazepam. These used to be the most commonly prescribed medicines for anxiety but can be addictive and can also make you drowsy. A short course of up to two to three weeks may be prescribed rather than long-term use.

Hydroxyzine. This is an antihistamine which is sometimes used to ease anxiety symptoms. A common side-effect though is drowsiness.

Pregabalin. This is a medication used for several conditions (principally epilepsy). It has been found to be useful in treating GAD. It tends to be considered for GAD if the other treatments mentioned above have been unhelpful.

NB the above is not an exhaustive list and should not be seen as replacement for advice from a medical practitioner.

▶ Cognitive behavioural therapy (CBT)

This is arguably the most effective treatment. It probably works for over half of people with GAD to reduce symptoms and improve quality of life. CBT is offered by many practitioners and works by looking at the interaction between thoughts (cognitions) and behaviours. It is based on the idea that how we think can affect how we feel and behave. The following techniques for self-help with GAD are based on CBT approaches.

Remember this

Cognitive behavioural therapy is probably the most effective treatment for generalized anxiety disorder.

▶ Anxiety diaries

Before we start trying to reduce general anxiety, it is important to be aware of exactly what is going on in terms of your anxiety.

Spend a few minutes thinking about the following questions:

▶ What makes you anxious?

▶ What do you do when you are anxious?

▶ How often do you get anxious?

▶ How long do you stay anxious for?

In order to fully answer these questions, it is useful to keep an anxiety diary as shown below.

Date/Time	What is making you anxious or triggering your anxiety?	What are you thinking?	How anxious do you feel on a scale of 0–100?	How long did the anxiety episode last?

Complete this diary for at least a week before going on to the next section.

Techniques to reduce anxiety

Now we'll look in detail at three techniques to help reduce your anxiety:

- Challenge unhelpful thinking styles.
- Manage the amount of 'worry' time.
- Learn to be more relaxed in general.

TECHNIQUE 1: CHALLENGE UNHELPFUL THINKING STYLES

Go back through your anxiety diary (above). What were you thinking? What was going through your mind? Use the following table to identify your unhelpful thinking styles.

What were you thinking?	Unhelpful thinking style
Were you imagining what might happen? Were you thinking about the possible outcomes of an event? Were you assuming that things would go badly for you?	**Predicting the future:** this is where we invest a lot of energy predicting what will happen – and usually these predictions are of dire consequences. Often things won't turn out as bad as we fear but we have wasted a lot of energy worrying about events that may never happen.
Did you think that another person would think badly of you? Did you guess that another person would judge you unfavourably?	**Mind-reading:** This is where you make assumptions about what other people are thinking without having any evidence to back this up.
Did you exaggerate how bad something was? Did you imagine that something you did/didn't do would have major consequences?	**Catastrophizing:** This is where you blow things out of proportion so that things seem to be worse than they really are.
Did you only notice the bad things that were happening/had happened? Did you focus on something negative that someone said?	**Focusing on the negative:** This is where you notice and focus on what went badly and ignore things that went well.
Did you feel annoyed because you should have done something differently? Did you feel angry with yourself for not behaving in a certain way?	**Should-ing:** This is where you get preoccupied with how you think things should be and not accepting how things really are.
Did you assume that because one thing happened, other similar things would be likely to happen? Did you worry that because something bad happened to you, other bad things would follow?	**Over-generalizing:** This is where you assume that an isolated incident is representative of all future events.
Did you worry about what would happen if... (e.g. if you had a panic attack, or if no one talked to you etc.).	**What ifs:** Being preoccupied with 'what if' scenarios can stop you doing things or going to places.
Did you make negative statements about yourself? Did you condemn yourself?	**Labelling:** this is where you give yourself a condemning label like 'I am stupid'.

Key idea

Identifying unhelpful thinking styles is an important first step to beating excessive anxiety.

Case study

Richard was a university student who was very anxious, in particular about participating in classes. He kept an anxiety diary to help him identify his unhelpful thinking and found that he ticked most of the boxes for the different categories of unhelpful thoughts. For example, some of his worries were connected with things that might happen (predicting the future) – he worried that if he spoke out or put his hand up, he would say something stupid and everyone would laugh at him. He realized that he was assuming that things would go badly for him. He also assumed that he knew what everyone else was thinking (mind-reading) because he was convinced that his class-mates thought he was dull and stupid. He always imagined really dire consequences (catastrophizing) of taking an active part in the classes too – he felt that if he got an answer wrong then everyone would think he was stupid and that this would make him the laughing stock of the entire campus. The diary helped him realize that even if he did get the answer wrong, the consequences wouldn't be as dramatic as he imagined.

When Richard did speak in class, he always noticed what he did wrong (focusing on the negative) and would become preoccupied with thinking about what he should have done (should-ing). For example, he would focus on the fact that he stuttered when he started, rather than on the fact that the lecturer praised him for his insight. He also tended to label himself as stupid (labelling) on the basis of one or two bad experiences (over-generalizing) – such as when he had got a question wrong at school years ago and everyone had laughed at him.

Now start a new diary (see opposite) for a further week, in which you specifically try to identify any unhelpful thinking styles. See the example diary entry to get you started.

Unhelpful thinking styles diary

Date/Time	What is making you anxious or triggering your anxiety?	What are you thinking?	What unhelpful thinking style are you using?
[Example] Thursday	My daughter asks for money for residential school trip	I can't cope with the demands for money. I might lose my job and then how would we cope? It is a struggle to pay for everything already; if I lose my job we could end up losing the house. My kids must already resent me for not earning enough.	Catastrophizing Mind-reading

Now that you have begun to identify your unhelpful thinking styles, you need to start *challenging* them. You can do this by asking yourself a series of questions about each unhelpful thought that you identify:

▶ **Questions to challenge unhelpful thinking**

1 Is there any evidence for this?

2 Are there any alternative explanations or viewpoints?

3 How important is this in the long-term (e.g. how will this affect me in five years?)

4 What would you advise someone else in this situation?

(See Chapter 10 for more on challenging unhelpful thinking in relation to depression.)

Mythbuster

Anxious people are often well able to advise other people on what to do in certain situations but seem unable to take the same advice themselves.

In answering these questions, you should be able to come up with more helpful thoughts with which to replace the unhelpful ones. You can now start a third type of anxiety diary and this is one that you can keep up for the longterm (until challenging your unhelpful thoughts and replacing them with more helpful ones becomes second nature).

Key idea

Challenge unhelpful thoughts by looking for evidence to back up what you believe and by searching for alternative explanations for what might have happened.

Challenging unhelpful thoughts diary

Situation/date	Unhelpful thoughts and category of unhelpful thought	Challenges to these thoughts	New, more helpful alternative thought

TECHNIQUE 2: MANAGE THE AMOUNT OF WORRY TIME

Anxious people tend to spend a lot of time worrying – and often go over and over the same things in their head. One way then to cope, is to try to reduce the amount of time that you spend engaged in 'worrying'. You can do this by scheduling 'worry time' at certain times of the day – and not allow yourself any worrying outside of these times. During your allotted 'worry time' you can write down your worries and try to either challenge them using the diaries above, or problem-solve using problem solving techniques (see the Try it now: box below).

Mythbuster

Managing your anxiety is not about trying to eliminate it – you are still allowed to worry, but the aim should be to make the worry more manageable.

Try it now: Problem-solving techniques

1 Identify and write down the problem.
2 Write down a list of possible solutions or options perhaps by brainstorming.
3 Write down the pros and cons of each possible solution.
4 Select a solution and see how you feel about it – this will help you to decide if it's the right one for you.
5 Consider the risks of making a wrong decision – often the consequences are not as dire as you might fear.

When your worry time is over, force yourself to stop worrying until your next worry session – this will allow you to consider your worries with fresh eyes which will help enormously, especially with putting worries into perspective.

Key idea

Learning problem-solving techniques can help you deal more effectively with some of your worries.

Initially, worry times could be for 15 minutes every two hours. As you get used to taking a break from your worries, you can increase the amount of time between worry-sessions. If you find yourself worrying in between sessions, try to stop yourself, perhaps by trying to do distracting things (see the Try it now box below) or just by forcing yourself to stop the worrying, safe in the knowledge that you can worry again soon! Jot down your worries in a special worry book so that you won't 'forget' to come back to them at the next scheduled worry session.

Try it now: Distracting yourself from your worries

* Count backwards in 11s from 5000.
* Plan supper.
* Write a shopping list.
* Try to notice five things in your surroundings that you can see, hear, smell and touch.
* Ring a friend.
* Look for five things that begin with the letter A, then B etc.

TECHNIQUE 3: LEARN HOW TO RELAX

Remember what happens to your body when you are anxious? See earlier in this chapter for a reminder! When you are relaxed the opposite happens, so if you can get your body to relax, you should be able to dramatically reduce your symptoms of anxiety. Your heart rate slows down, you breathe slower and more deeply, your muscles relax, and your blood pressure lowers. Since it's impossible to be anxious and relaxed at the same time, strengthening your body's relaxation response is a powerful anxiety-relieving tactic. Your aim then, should be to try to introduce relaxing activities into your day so as to increase the amount of time that your body is relaxed. Some people feel guilty about taking time out to just 'chill', but it is essential for your mental health so shouldn't be regarded as 'wasting time'.

A good way to do this is to start to keep a relaxation diary (see below), in which you try to make sure that each day you schedule in a relaxation activity or two. This could be something that you find relaxing, such as reading, having a bath, walking, watching TV etc. Or it could be a relaxation exercise (see the progressive muscle relaxation technique opposite).

Relaxation diary

Date	Relaxation technique	Length of time

Progressive muscle relaxation (PMR) is a proven technique that can help you release muscle tension and reduce the physical symptoms associated with anxiety (such as raised blood pressure). It helps to slow your breathing rate down and to learn when your body is showing signs of anxiety. PMR is a technique that needs to be learned and which takes time to have an impact, but if you practise it for 20 minutes every day, it can be very effective.

Try it now: Progressive muscle relaxation therapy

This technique helps the user to learn the difference between tension in the body, and relaxation. Many relaxation techniques rely on telling people to 'relax' but this is actually quite hard to do. Progressive muscle relaxation works by teaching you to tense each muscle in turn, and then to relax it, so that you can really feel the difference between tension and relaxation. Try it for yourself.

1 Sit comfortably in an armchair or you can even lie on the bed. Close your eyes for best effect (but not if it makes you uncomfortable).
2 Concentrate on your breathing – breathe in and out really slowly. Every time you breathe out, say to yourself the word 'relax'. Do this several times.
3 Now start with your toes. Curl and tense your toes tightly so that it feels very uncomfortable. Notice how tensing your toes makes your calves and even your thighs uncomfortable too. Notice how tensing just your toes can spread the tension through your body. Now, relax your toes and enjoy the feeling of relaxation this produces. Notice the difference between tension in your toes and relaxation. And, every time you breathe out, say to yourself the word 'relax'.
4 Repeat.
5 Now move on to your thighs. Tense your thighs tightly so that it feels very uncomfortable. Notice how tensing your thighs spreads the tension throughout your body – your tummy feels tense, even your

arms. Now, relax your thighs and enjoy the feeling of relaxation and warmth that this produces. Notice the difference between tension in your thighs and relaxation. And, every time you breathe out, say to yourself the word 'relax'.

6 Repeat.

7 Now move on to your stomach. Tense your tummy tightly so that it feels very uncomfortable. Notice how tensing your stomach muscles spreads the tension throughout your body. Now, relax your tummy and enjoy the feeling of relaxation and warmth that this produces. Notice the difference between tension in your tummy and relaxation. And, every time you breathe out, say to yourself the word 'relax'.

8 Repeat.

9 Repeat this tensing and relaxing of each muscle group in turn: your fingers (clench into tight fists); shoulders (shrug them to your neck); eyes (squeeze them tightly closed); and face (scrunch up your mouth). Finally, tense your whole body and relax it.

FURTHER TIPS TO REDUCE ANXIETY

1 Build a strong support system. Know who you can talk to about your worries – if you are short on a support network, think about building friendships by socializing, joining clubs etc. Be careful though – don't start offloading your worries as soon as you meet someone, or talking too much about your problems. If you do this, people will soon start avoiding you and you will become even more isolated. But, if your worries do seem to be getting out of control, talking to a trusted friend or family member can help put things in perspective.

2 Equally, know who to avoid when you're feeling anxious. Some people are known as 'anxiety importers' – they end up making people around them feel anxious. These people feed your anxieties and make you feel worse. Rather than reassure you, they may even give you extra things to worry about. Learn to identify such people and avoid them.

3 A healthy, balanced lifestyle plays a big role in keeping the symptoms of generalized anxiety disorder (GAD) at bay. Adopting healthy eating habits can help; regular meals can help you to avoid low blood sugar, which can make you feel anxious and irritable. Eating plenty of complex carbohydrates such as whole grains, fruits and vegetables can not only stabilize blood sugar levels, but can also boost serotonin, a neurotransmitter with calming effects on your body. Limit caffeine and refined sugar too: caffeine can increase anxiety and interfere with sleep while sugar can cause blood sugar levels to spike and then crash, leaving you feeling emotionally and physically drained.

4 Exercise regularly: exercise is a natural and effective anti-anxiety treatment. Aerobic exercise relieves tension and stress, boosts physical and mental energy, and enhances well-being through the release of endorphins, the brain's feel-good chemicals.

5 Avoid alcohol and nicotine: alcohol temporarily reduces anxiety and worry, but it actually causes anxiety symptoms as it wears off. While it may seem like cigarettes are calming, nicotine is actually a powerful stimulant. Smoking leads to higher, not lower, levels of anxiety.

Mythbuster

Alcohol might seem to help with worries but can actually make your anxiety worse in the long term.

6 Finally, try to get enough sleep. Anxiety and worry can cause sleep problems, but lack of sleep can also contribute to anxiety. When you're sleep deprived, your ability to handle anxiety and tension is compromised.

Focus points

✻ It is normal to feel anxious when we feel threatened but excessive anxiety can occur when we feel anxious for too long or feel it too intensely.

✻ Anxiety can be very debilitating even without associated conditions such as panic attacks or phobias accompanying it.

✻ Cognitive behavioural therapy can be extremely effective in treating anxiety and the first step is often identifying unhelpful thoughts.

✻ Unhelpful thoughts are those characteristic patterns of thinking that add to and maintain anxiety; they are formed by habit and as such can take effort to break.

✻ Challenging unhelpful thoughts coupled with other relaxation techniques can be really effective in beating anxiety.

4

Dealing with phobias

In this chapter you will learn:

- ► *About the avoidance–fear cycle*
- ► *A six-step programme to tackle your phobia*
- ► *What some of the barriers to effective treatment are*

Treating your phobia

So, now we know what phobias are, how do we go about treating them?
The techniques described in this chapter are cognitive behavioural
techniques and are thought to be the most effective at curing phobias.
They are based on a six-step treatment programme (see Figure 4.1):

▶ Step 1: Knowledge acquisition

Knowledge is a powerful first weapon to use against phobias.
You should educate yourself firstly about the nature of phobias
(see Chapter 1) because this will help you to understand what is
happening in your body and what will happen to you while you
are facing your fears. Quite simply, our bodies cannot maintain the
acute level of fear experienced at first during a phobic encounter
and the fear will (as long as we don't escape) eventually subside.

This is like being on a roller-coaster ride; the first time we go on
it is terrifying but we soon 'get used to it' and find it less scary
the second time. By the tenth time, we might wonder why on
earth it was so scary the first time! This is called habituation
and our bodies are designed to habituate to scary things that are
not actually harming us – this is because, once our bodies can
see that the threat is not dangerous, we need to stop diverting
energy to being scared of it because we might need to conserve
that energy in case something even scarier comes along.

Remember that a phobia is an *irrational* fear (see Chapter 1) so the whole point of it is that it isn't really dangerous – but we are reacting as if it is dangerous.

Thus, our fear when encountering the source of our phobia might be very strong but, assuming that we do not actually get harmed, the fear will fade. We will not collapse, have a heart attack or die. As long as we do not escape, we will simply get used to the fear and the fear will fade. If we do escape, we won't habituate or get used to the panic and the fear will keep coming back. This knowledge should sustain us during an attack.

Figure 4.1 The six-step treatment programme

Figure 4.2 shows how someone's fear might pan out if they don't attempt to escape from the situation. It shows how the fear rises dramatically from time point 1 to time point 3 (when they encounter the source of their phobia). After that, the fear diminishes, though it does rise again every so often – but not as high as the first 'spike'. Each fear spike is, in theory, slightly lower than the last, until the general level of fear drops and the person has *habituated* or got used to the fearful situation.

Remember this

If you don't run away or try to escape, the fear will subside eventually.

Compare this to what might happen if the person escapes at time point 3 – i.e. when the fear is very bad. Figure 4.3 shows how the fear will totally disappear once the person escapes (time point 4) but each time they subsequently face the source of their phobia, the fear spikes again to levels as high as that first exposure. In other words, if you keep escaping, you will never habituate and the fear will always remain as high. You will never conquer your phobia.

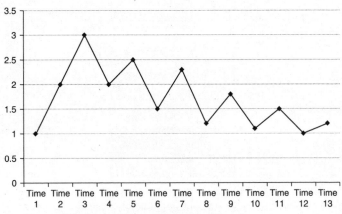

Figure 4.2 Habituation of our fear when we do not escape

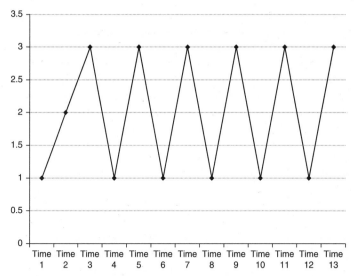

Figure 4.3 The fear response never weakens if we escape

The second area of knowledge to acquire is in relation to your own specific phobia. Learning about the source of your fear is important. For example, if you are afraid of lifts, a thorough understanding of how lifts operate, what happens when they fail, how long before occupants might be rescued etc., can be very helpful (see Julia's case study below). Fear of flying can be helped by gaining an understanding of how planes stay in the air and what all those noises mean when you are airborne (for more on this see Chapter 7). In Chapter 7 when we discuss specific phobias, we will talk about how and where such knowledge might be obtained but for the purposes of this chapter it might be useful to do your own research either by asking experts (see Julia's case study) or by obtaining statistical information via the internet or books.

Key idea

Find out all you can about your phobia, especially information about the risk or dangers involved or how you might cope if a feared consequence did happen.

Case study

Julie was very afraid of lifts and after the first session at my clinic, her 'homework' task was to find out about the lifts that she was going to try to use. The lifts she was going to start on were in a local shopping centre and she went along to customer services and explained her predicament. They were surprisingly understanding and put her in touch with the engineers who maintained the lifts. They explained how rarely modern lifts of this kind break down and what happens if someone presses the emergency button – how long it takes to respond etc. She discovered that these lifts even have back-up generators in case of power failure but if they do break down, it takes about an hour for help to arrive. This took away a great deal of fear of the unknown and put her in a better position to start trying to overcome her fears.

Try it now

Write down your own research findings about your own phobia.

▶ Step 2: Create your hierarchy

At this point, you need to establish clearly what you are phobic about and what you are not. This sounds obvious – for example, if you have a lift phobia, you might say that 'I am phobic about lifts. I am not phobic about escalators'. However, it is not quite as simple as this. When a lift phobic presents at my clinic, these are the questions I ask them:

▶ Do all lifts scare you as much?

▶ Have you ever been in a lift?

▶ Can you go in lifts with other people?

▶ Are there some people who you would find it easier to be in a lift with than others?

- Are small lifts the same to you as large lifts?

- Can you go in glass lifts?

- Would going to the tenth floor be as bad as the first floor?

- Can you go near a lift?

Similarly, I would ask someone with a dog phobia:

- Do all dogs scare you as much as each other?

- Are you as scared of small dogs as big dogs?

- Are dogs on leads as bad as dogs not on leads?

- Can you walk in a park if there are dogs there?

- Do you need to cross the road to avoid a dog?

- Does looking at pictures of dogs alarm you?

- Could you look at a dog through a window?

- Could you watch a tape of dogs?

Now it's your turn. Write down questions you could ask about your own phobia (see overleaf). Once you have asked the questions, you can start to develop your own 'hierarchy of feared situations'. This simply means that you rate all the situations you have listed above on a scale of 0–100, where 0 means that this holds no fear for you whatsoever, and 100 means that this situation is unimaginably terrifying.

You then need to arrange your feared situations in a 'ladder' so that the situations that are easiest for you to imagine doing are at the bottom of the ladder, and the situations that are the hardest for you to imagine being able to do are at the top. The situations at the bottom of the ladder should be those that you think you could manage to do right away, without much difficulty at all.

What questions can you ask about your own phobia?

Question 1

Question 2

Question 3

Question 4

Question 5

Question 6

Question 7

Question 8

Question 9

Question 10

. . . .

A sample hierarchy ladder for a lift phobic then, might look like this (obviously, this will vary for each individual):

Step 1: Go near a lift.

Step 2: Step into, then immediately out of, a glass lift that only goes up or down one floor.

Step 3: Stay in a glass lift while going up or down one floor, when there are other people present.

Step 4: Stay in a glass lift while going up or down one floor, when there are no other people present.

Step 5: Step into, then immediately out of, a large lift in a busy place that only goes up or down one floor.

Step 6: Stay in a large lift in a busy place while going up or down one floor, when there are other people present.

Step 7: Go up two floors in a large lift in a busy place when there are other people present.

Step 8: Go up three floors in a large lift in a busy place when there are other people present.

Step 9: Go up ten floors in large lift in a busy place when there are other people present.

Step 10: Go up two floors in large lift in a busy place when there are no other people present.

Step 11: Go up ten floors in large lift in a busy place when there are no other people present.

Step 12: Use a small lift in a busy place when there are other people present.

Step 13: Use a small lift in a busy place when there are no other people present.

Step 14: Use a small lift in a quiet location when there are other people present.

Step 15: Use a small lift in a quiet location when there are no other people present.

In this case, the lift phobic is afraid that she might get stuck in the lift, so glass lifts are easier to imagine using than non-glass lifts because she can see out and summon help if required. Larger lifts feel safer as do lifts in which there are other people. She might also feel safer in lifts where there are clear instructions on what to do in case of breakdown. Different people might have different fears, however, so no two hierarchies will be identical.

Now create your own hierarchy using the following template.

	Task or situation
1	
2	
3	
4	
5	
6	
7	
8	
9	

▶ Step 3: Challenge your negative thoughts

While you are working your way through the *behavioural* programme as set out in Step 2, it is important to also work on the thoughts that you are having which are feeding your fears – this is the *cognitive* element of the programme.

Remember this
Thinking errors can be responsible for feeding or maintaining your phobia.

Some of this is similar in approach to that outlined in Chapter 3 (on anxiety). Your first task is to actually identify what you are thinking when faced with your feared situation, or when even imagining facing your feared situation.

For example, if you are phobic about flying, your thought processes when you get on a plane (or imagine getting on a plane) might go something like this:

This plane might crash.

I am trapped in this plane.

I won't be able to get out if I have to.

I will have a panic attack mid-air and won't be able to escape.

I might die from my panic attack.

I will make a fool of myself.

A lot of these thoughts or *cognitions* are based on the sort of thinking errors outlined in Chapter 3 (and examined in relation to depression in Chapter 10). Thinking errors are simply flaws in your thinking; the most common thinking errors or flaws with regards to phobias can be summarized as follows:

Common thinking error	Example
Predicting the future	This is where you predict what will happen during the phobic response, e.g. 'the plane will crash', 'I will die', 'I will have a panic attack'.
Catastrophizing	This is where you blow reactions to the phobia out of proportion so that things seem to be worse than they really are, e.g. 'if I have a panic attack I will die' or 'the noise in the engine means the place will crash'.
Over-generalizing	This is where you assume that an isolated phobic response is representative of all future events. However, just because you once had a panic attack on a plane doesn't mean you that you will again. Or just because a plane crashed four years ago, that doesn't signify that yours will crash.
Mind-reading	This is where you assume you know what other people are thinking in relation to any outward displays or signs of your phobia: 'if I have a panic attack on the plane everyone will think I am mad'.

Once you have caught yourself making these thinking errors, the next step is to start challenging them, perhaps by looking at the evidence to support your cognitions.

Ask yourself:

▶ Is there any evidence that contradicts this thought?

▶ Can I do anything to prevent this from happening?

▶ What would I advise a friend in this situation?

Key idea

Being aware of what you are thinking, and whether you are making thinking errors, is a vital part of curing your phobia.

It's also helpful to come up with some positive coping statements that you can tell yourself when facing your phobia. For example:

▶ 'I've felt this way before and nothing terrible happened. It may be unpleasant, but it won't harm me.'

▶ 'There is no evidence that what I fear will happen.'

▶ 'I know that nothing dangerous will happen to me.'

▶ 'If the worst happens and I have a panic attack I'll simply wait for it to pass.'

▶ 'I've flown many times and the plane has never crashed. In fact, I don't know anyone who's ever been in a plane crash. Statistically, flying is very safe.'

This plane might crash.

The statistics on plane disasters show that crashes are actually very rare.

I am trapped in this plane.

So what? I don't need to get out until we land!

I won't be able to get out if I have to.

But I don't have to unless there is an emergency and this is highly unlikely and rare.

I will have a panic attack mid-air and won't be able to escape.

If i have a panic attack I will just have to ride it out – nothing will happen to me.

I might die from my panic attack.

People don't die from panic attacks.

I will make a fool of myself.

No one will notice even if I have a panic attack.

▶ Step 4: Learn relaxation techniques

Remember what happens to your body when you are anxious or fearful? As explained in Chapter 3, as our anxiety rises, a range of hormones are produced that affect every part of our body in one way or another. These 'fear' hormones are similar to those released when we are stressed.

Adrenaline causes the heart to beat faster and blood pressure to rise; this allows oxygen-rich blood to flow more quickly to the areas of the body that are responsible for reacting to the source of anxiety. These areas are those that need extra energy – for example, the arms (to fight) or the legs (to flee) and the brain (to think quickly).

All this anticipated extra activity requires extra energy and the other important hormone, *cortisol*, is responsible for this bit of the fear reaction. The release of cortisol in the blood causes the liver to convert its emergency stores of energy (in the form of glycogen) into the more readily usable form of glucose. This extra glucose provides the surge of energy needed to beat the source of the fear.

The net effect of all this activity is a rapid heartbeat, breathlessness (as the lungs struggle to take in more oxygen), raised blood pressure (hypertension) and a raised body temperature (due to using more energy). All this made our frightened ancestors ideally placed to deal with the sources of their fear by either fighting them or running away.

When we face our phobias, we are in a different position. We can easily reduce the fear and symptoms of fear (that are, in themselves, very frightening) by escaping (running away) but all that happens then is that we get into a avoidance–fear cycle as outlined in Chapter 3. Instead, we are trying to retrain the brain to stay and face the fear, so if we can try to physically relax our bodies then we will be able to minimize some of the terrifying symptoms of our fear.

When you are relaxed, the opposite of the above reactions happen, so if you can get your body to relax, you should be able to dramatically reduce your fearful symptoms. When we are relaxed, our heart rate slows down, we breathe slower and more deeply, our muscles relax, and our blood pressure lowers. Since it's impossible to be overly fearful and anxious, and relaxed at the same time, strengthening your body's relaxation response is a powerful fear-reducing tactic.

The relaxation techniques that were outlined in Chapter 3 can be used here, but in this case, they are also to be used when attempting to carry out Step 5 below (when you face the source of your phobia). As you get accustomed to using the progressive muscle relaxation technique you will be able to do a shortened version of it (see Chapter 5) whenever you are really anxious. You will eventually learn to become aware of when your body is getting tense and to be able to relax very quickly. This will minimize the symptoms of fear and of the chances of them progressing to a full-blown panic attack. You should wait until you have completed your relaxation exercises before attempting the next step on your ladder (see Step 5).

Key idea

Learning to switch on relaxation when you are very fearful can really help reduce the feelings of anxiety and their symptoms.

▶ Step 5: Desensitization or self-exposure

Now you are ready for the next step 'in vivo (real-life) exposure'. By this stage, you are following the plan that you set out in Step 2. You simply start at the lowest level of your hierarchy and work your way up (using the skills to challenge your thinking and the relaxation techniques that you have learned so far). For each rung on your ladder, you should give yourself an anxiety score (i.e. before, during and after) – and you repeat the same step until you reduce your anxiety levels so they are manageable.

Most of the time, you will probably find that your anxiety score before the event is actually higher than during the feared event. It is the anticipation that is often the worse. Realizing this (through experience) is a vital breakthrough – the fear of the event is often worse than the event itself.

Keep a record of your experiences, using the following template.

Date	Step/activity	Score 0–100 (pre, during and post)	Thoughts	Thinking errors?

Each step may take several sessions to achieve. Your scores will need to come down to around 20 before you are ready to move on to the next rung. This means that you will need to repeat the stage over and over again, often across several days. You should give yourself breaks between attempts and use the relaxation and thought-stopping techniques in Steps 3 and 4.

If possible, it can be a good idea to have a trusted friend to accompany you as you undertake your in vivo practice. They can remind you of the techniques in Steps 3 and 4 and help you to gauge your scores and levels of anxiety.

Remember this

Each step on the hierarchy should be approached slowly and the next step should not be attempted until anxiety levels from the previous step are manageable.

Case study

Kai had been afraid of spiders ever since he was small and he remembered the incident that started the fear; he had been walking in a park and holding onto a rail when he suddenly felt a spider crawl over his hand. This gave him a terrible fright and he became afraid of spiders after that.

But lately, his fear has developed so much that it was taking over his life. He couldn't go anywhere where he might encounter spiders – this meant that parks were out, but also many rooms in his house were out of bounds, especially the bathroom. He had to check for spiders everywhere he went and before he went to bed he would examine his room carefully. He would only visit the houses of a few friends that he felt were safe, but the problem was even more severe in that he couldn't look at pictures of spiders or even talk about them without having intense panic attacks. Halloween was a very difficult time of year because of all the spider displays in shops, adverts on TV, in magazines etc. He became a virtual recluse at that time of year, sometimes not even going in to work.

Kai developed his hierarchical ladder and at the bottom of the list was mentioning the word 'spider'. He tackled this first. He made a tape of himself saying the word over and over and he played it for a few minutes a day. Eventually he progressed to playing it for half an hour a time and before long, the word stopped provoking anxiety in him. At this point, he told his family to try to mention the word spider whenever they could until he got used to that too.

He then moved on the next rung on his ladder which was pictures of spiders. He started with a picture that he placed at the far end of the room and waited until is panic subsided before moving a bit closer to the picture. He eventually progressed to holding the picture.

In this way he was able to move slowly up his hierarchical ladder until he could live a normal life again.

▶ Step 6: Distraction

Building in your own distraction strategies can provide an excellent crutch for you if things start to get difficult. Distractors will vary from person to person and from situation to situation. For example, I had a client with a choking phobia who found that drinking helped her to cope with the choking sensation; she learned to carry a carton of drink around with her. I have found that a carton of drink is very effective for many people who experience panic in phobic situations – the act of opening the drink and swallowing it can help to distract from their fears. I had one client with a driving phobia who would never get in a car without carrying a drink – when she had one, she felt safe. It was just a crutch, but it worked.

Another good distractor is chewing gum. Some studies have suggested that chewing gum when anxious can reduce cortisol secretion which helps to reduce anxiety (Sketchley-Kaye, et al, 2011). These researchers even suggest the best flavour to optimize these anxiety-reducing benefits – peppermint! The act of unwrapping and chewing gum can in itself be a good distractor and being aware of the added anxiety-reducing benefit can add to the calming effect. So, making sure that you carry chewing gum can be a wise move.

If you are phobic in certain situations then taking something to do or read can be an effective distractor. Newspapers, iPods, phones, Kindles etc. can help you to distract yourself in difficult situations.

Of course, these distractors can lead to a situation whereby the person becomes reliant on them and can only function with them. I think this is a small price to pay (e.g. remembering to carry chewing gum) although it could mean that failure to bring along the distractor can lead to panic – but at least it means that the person can function well most of the time. Eventually, the distractors, rather like comfort blankets with toddlers, become less and less important and most people will be able to reduce their reliance on them.

Barriers to effective treatment

The above treatment programme might not always be successful and there are a number of reasons for this, or barriers to successful treatment.

THE PHOBIA IS COMPLEX

The treatment programme outlined in this chapter works best for specific or simple phobias (see Chapter 1). If you are trying to treat more complex phobias such as social phobia, you should refer to Chapter 6).

OTHER COMPLICATIONS

Sometimes people with phobias have other mental health issues that can interfere with successful treatment programmes. Some of these are outlined briefly in Chapter 3, but depression is one very common, co-occurring condition that can make following a phobia treatment programme as described in this chapter very difficult indeed. Non-compliance rates are very high and it is notoriously difficult to motivate yourself to do the in vivo exercises if you are depressed.

In this case, it is recommended that you see a professional who might advise medication, and they can also help you through the cognitive behavioural programme as outlined here (see also Chapter 10 on depression).

People who are very severely anxious in general (see Chapter 3) might also have difficult completing this programme, especially if they are already working on the exercises in Chapter 3. In this case, it might be wise to try to reduce your general anxiety by using the techniques in the previous chapter, before attempting to tackle specific phobias too. Medication prescribed in conjunction with cognitive behavioural techniques can also be helpful, so seeing a medical practitioner might be useful in such cases.

UNWILLINGNESS TO DO IN VIVO TASKS

If you find that you are simply not willing to do the tasks then it could be that you are not motivated enough to change or that you are trying to go too quickly or to push too hard beyond your comfort zone. If you are not motivated enough, even the tasks at the bottom of your hierarchy will seem daunting and it will be easier to just give up. Similarly, you can become de-motivated by lack of progress or by the feeling that you have too much to accomplish before making progress; this can be the case, for example, when you have a hierarchical ladder containing around 20 steps and each step seems to be taking a few weeks to achieve.

Rest assured that slow progress at the start does not mean progress will remain slow. I have seen many clients with very long hierarchical lists who think it will take them years to get through; a breakthrough often happens after a few steps at which point progress suddenly becomes a lot faster. Thus, for example, a lift phobic might have taken four weeks to be able to go two floors in a large lift, but only a week to tick off all the remaining steps in their ladder.

The trick is to go at a pace that you feel comfortable with and not try to rush through the steps. If you move up a rung before you have really conquered the previous one, then this can cause too much anxiety too quickly which can lead to unwillingness to continue.

SETBACKS

Having a bad experience can set you back and make you reluctant to carry on. For example, a client who is afraid of dogs might be progressing well, but then encounters a fierce dog who jumps on him on the beach; this can frighten him so much that he feels that he is back to square one and has to start at the bottom of his hierarchy again.

However, it is rare that all progress made is totally lost in these cases. Even a return to the bottom of the ladder is not a catastrophe and progress will usually be much swifter than it was the first time.

Remember this

If the programme you have devised with the help of this chapter is not going well, it might be that you need the support of an experienced practitioner to guide you through it.

Flooding

A word here about 'flooding' techniques which some therapists will offer (they will advertise 'your phobia cured in one hour' etc.). This is where there is extreme exposure to the feared situation. If you were afraid of spiders for example, flooding would involve you going straight to the top of your hierarchy (which might be holding a tarantula in a zoo). A lift phobic who wanted to try 'flooding', might force himself to go into a small secluded lift that goes up 20 floors.

Flooding can be a very fast technique and some have boasted that it has a success rate of over 50 per cent. However, this is actually quite a low success rate compared with a much higher rate with the six-step programme outlined above. And, it can backfire horribly. Having said that, I have used the flooding approach on occasion with height phobic clients with great success; I use an indoor high-wire adventure centre which height phobic clients can progress to using. Sometimes, a client wants to go straight to the top of their hierarchy by starting with the high rope bridges, and this can work well if the client is motivated to use this technique. But, such flooding should be used with care and only under the supervision of an experienced therapist.

Mythbuster

Going straight to the top of your hierarchy might seem a good way to cure your phobia quickly but it can have disastrous consequences. It is safer and more effective to go up the rungs of your ladder slowly.

If you decide that you are too impatient to go through your full hierarchy, you might find that the anxiety provoked by going straight to the top is too much to bear. This can even lead you to experience post-traumatic stress disorder (see Chapter 9) and can leave you worse off than before. So, it is best to be patient, take your time and work through the schedule at a manageable pace; never be tempted to rush things!

Focus points

* Understanding how phobias affect our bodies and having a good knowledge of your own phobia can be an important first step to conquering it (see Chapter 7 too on specific phobias).
* Creating a hierarchy of feared situations means that you can tackle those situations that are going to be more manageable first – and you will also have attainable goals to aim for during the programme.
* Remember to move up the ladder slowly and take your time; the programme could take several weeks to accomplish.
* Some people will have difficulty completing the programme on their own and should seek the input of an experienced professional. If you do have difficulties, it doesn't mean that the programme isn't right – it could just mean that, for various reasons, you can't do it easily on your own.
* The keys to success are patience, keeping diaries and taking it slowly!

5

Dealing with panic attacks

In this chapter you will learn:

- ▶ *A seven-step programme for overcoming panic attacks*
- ▶ *How to cope with nocturnal panic attacks and performance anxiety*
- ▶ *About the difficulties you may experience in tackling your panic attacks*

How do you feel?

1 Do you do all you can to avoid getting panic attacks?   Yes/No

2 Do you worry about going into situations where you might get a panic attack?   Yes/No

3 When you have a panic attack, do you worry about what will happen to you?   Yes/No

4 Do you normally try to escape as soon as you feel panicky? Yes/No

5 Do thoughts of panic attacks tend to occupy you a lot of the time?   Yes/No

If you answer 'yes' to more than a couple of these questions, then this chapter is for you.

Combating panic attacks

When panic attacks hit, they are devastating and very hard to cope with. They are so uncomfortable that the desire to escape can be all-encompassing. The sufferer knows that only by escaping, will the panic subside.

This is indeed true to some extent; by escaping the situation where the panic attack is occurring, the panic will go. However, the panic attack will return, as strong as ever, should the sufferer go back to the situation where they became panicky. What's more, the fear of having another panic attack is so great, that they start to avoid any place or situation which might give rise to a panic attack.

All this leads to a cycle of fear and avoidance as sufferers start to avoid ever more places or situations out of fear of having a panic attack (see Chapter 2 for more on this).

In order to beat panic attacks, the answer is not, then, to escape from situations when you have a panic attack, but to stay and weather the storm. It is only by staying and learning you can survive the attack, that the fear of them will start to subside. And remember, it is fear of the panic attack that is actually causing the panic. When you stop fearing them, they will stop coming!

But, how can you break the cycle and learn to stop fearing panic attacks? Follow this seven-step programme to beat panic attacks:

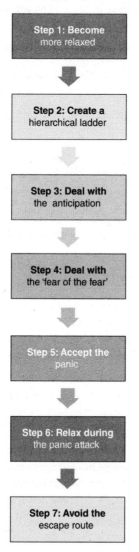

Step 1: Become
more relaxed

Step 2: Create a
hierarchical ladder

Step 3: Deal with
the anticipation

Step 4: Deal with
the 'fear of the fear'

Step 5: Accept the
panic

Step 6: Relax during
the panic attack

Step 7: Avoid the
escape route

▶ Step 1: Become more relaxed

If you are generally anxious, this can be a precursor to developing panic attacks or having another attack. This is because anxious individuals tend to be more threat-sensitive and aware of what can go wrong – they are more fearful in general. This can make them vulnerable to panic attacks. Their high levels of anxiety can also lead to physical symptoms (see Chapter 3) which can be misinterpreted in catastrophic ways (such as 'I am going to have a heart attack') – leading to panic attacks (caused by the fear of the fear). Thus, lowering general levels of anxiety is the first step to treating other anxiety-related conditions.

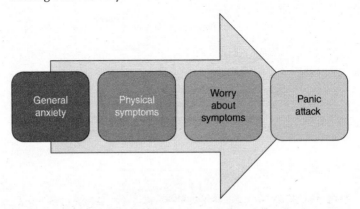

General anxiety → Physical symptoms → Worry about symptoms → Panic attack

Remember this

Lowering general anxiety levels will reduce your chances of having panic attacks.

The first step, then, is to become a less anxious person. Obviously, this is difficult, given that these could be habits of a lifetime and also given that the fear of having panic attacks is contributing to the general high levels of anxiety. Chapter 3 goes into greater detail about how to lower general anxiety levels but a brief reminder of the key points in relation to panic attacks is useful here too:

1   Challenge unhelpful thinking. While Chapter 3 goes into great depth about unhelpful thinking styles, it is worth challenging your thoughts about panic attacks in particular. For example,

there are many unhelpful thoughts you might have about panic attacks that are feeding your anxiety; try to replace these with new thoughts based on your new knowledge and awareness from Chapters 2 and 3. See the examples below:

Your turn:

My unhelpful thoughts	Replace with....

Key idea

Learn to challenge your negative thoughts about panic attacks by replacing unhelpful thoughts with more helpful ones.

2 In addition to the cognitive approaches (above), it is important to learn to relax your body so that you will have fewer symptoms of anxiety to start the whole panic attack cycle. Learning to relax your muscles will keep the terrifying anxiety symptoms to a minimum. This will reduce the chances of panic arising and also of your worrying about symptoms and catastrophizing them (e.g. imagining that you will faint or vomit). Use the progressive muscle relaxation technique outlined in Chapter 3. Learn to practise this several times a day and certainly before you are going out into a situation that might make you anxious or where you are fearful of having a panic attack.

▶ Step 2: Create a hierarchical ladder

Now you are ready to start facing your fears by deliberately going into a situation that might provoke a panic attack.

Just like the treatment programme for phobias in Chapter 4, here you will need to develop a hierarchical ladder of panic-inducing situations. If going to busy places is what causes panic attacks, you will need to create a hierarchy of those 'busy places' that are scary and those that are easier to cope with (see Chapter 4 for a reminder on how to create hierarchies).

Create your own hierarchy using the following template:

Step	Task or situation	Score 0–100 BEFORE	Score 0–100 DURING	Score 0–100 AFTER
1				
2				
3				
4				
5				
6				
7				
8				
9				

For some people, the hierarchy might not include a range of situations, but one situation broken down into steps. Imagine that you are fearful of having a panic attack on a bus (because you had one there in the past). Your hierarchical ladder might look like this:

Step	Task or situation	Score 0–100 BEFORE	Score 0–100 DURING	Score 0–100 AFTER
1	Walk to bus stop			
2	Wait at bus stop			
3	Stop a bus and talk to driver			
4	Get on bus for one stop with a trusted friend			
5	Get on bus for one stop with trusted friend, cross road and get on bus for return stop			
6	Repeat steps 4 and 5 but alone, perhaps with friend meeting me at bus stop			
7	Now go two stops with friend			
8	Now go three stops alone – perhaps have friend waiting to meet me or on other end of mobile phone			
9	Repeat with more and more stops			

You are now ready to start working your way up your hierarchy. As you can see from the example above, the plan is to start with easier, more manageable tasks and work your way up to the harder ones. The aim is not, as many people mistakenly believe, to ensure that you don't experience any panic attacks. The aim is to actually experience the attacks but to learn that you can manage and cope with them. As mentioned at the start of this chapter, while you are afraid of panic attacks, they will not be beaten – it is only when you are no longer afraid of panic that the fear of panic will go. At this point you will find that the attacks disappear too.

Mythbuster

Avoiding situations that give rise to panic will only solve the problem in the short term; in the long term, it is only by repeatedly exposing yourself to these situations that will stop the panic attacks.

The aim then is to go through the hierarchy while learning to cope with the panic that is produced. Many people feel that if they get on the bus and have a panic attack, they have 'failed' and the programme is not working. The opposite is true; if you manage to do all the tasks on the hierarchy without a single panic attack, then you have not learned to deal with them.

Remember this

When you start exposing yourself to the things that cause you to panic, start slowly with the situations which are easiest to cope with.

At this stage then, we are turning all your previous ideas on their head. You are no longer trying to avoid the panic! You are now actively trying to have panic attacks – but in manageable 'bite-size' stages. Coping with the attacks is the key here, and the next few steps will show you how to cope with them so that you no longer fear them.

▶ Step 3: Deal with the anticipation

Now that you are generally more relaxed (and don't go onto Step 2 of the programme until you *are* more relaxed – use the material in Chapter 3 to help you), you are ready to start facing your fears. Quite often, the anxiety about the possibility of panicking is often worse than the panic itself and this anxiety is often driven by *anticipation*. Anticipating the panic is likely to produce a great deal of anxiety which can lead to symptoms and greater panic:

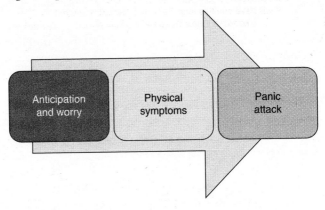

The anticipation leads to worry because of the thoughts that tend to go through the mind when anticipating a fearful event. It is likely that you will be thinking along the following lines:

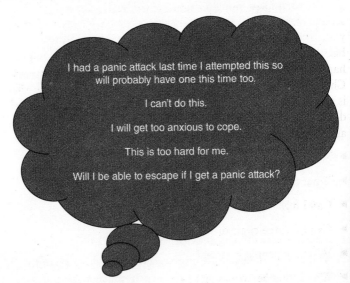

Write your thoughts down and try to replace them with more positive thoughts such as:

Just because I had a panic attack last time doesn't mean I will have one this time. Last time I wasn't prepared, knowledgeable or aware like I am now.

I can do this!

I will be able to cope.

It won't be too hard for me; plenty of people have beaten panic attacks so why shouldn't I?

I won't need to escape – a panic attack won't harm me and escaping will only make things worse.

Try not to indulge thoughts about what *could* happen (see section on unhelpful thinking styles in Chapter 3). Try to focus your thoughts on what you are doing now and don't look back at what happened in the past, nor forward at what might happen in the future ('predicting the future' thinking error – see Chapter 3). Focusing on your immediate surroundings and what is going on around you can help you to 'stay in the present' and distract you from worries about the past or future. For example, ask yourself the following questions:

▸ What can I hear?

▸ What can I see – what colours?

▸ Can I feel any different textures?

▸ Can I feel the chair or the ground?

▸ What are people wearing?

▸ Why is that person smiling?

At the same time, practise your relaxation skills (see Step 1 and Chapter 3) so that you are physically able to calm yourself down.

Remember this

Anticipating an uncomfortable event can be worse than the event itself.

Sometimes people will find the anticipation stage just too much to cope with and will back out and not progress to Step 3. Often they will come up with a range of excuses or reasons as to why they should not go through with the feared event at this time; for example, 'I feel a bit under the weather today – best wait until I feel better', or 'the weather is so bad today – I should wait for a drier day to go out' etc. Sometimes these excuses are valid (if you are really unwell, it probably is wise to wait until you feel better), but if you find yourself making too many excuses and putting off Step 3 for a long time, then perhaps you need support from an experienced professional.

▶ Step 4: Deal with the 'fear of the fear'

'Fear of the fear' is about being afraid of the worrying thoughts associated with your panic. If we experienced the symptoms of panic attacks but were able to label them as something harmless, then we would not 'fear the fear'. We would simply accept that the feelings are uncomfortable, but the panic wouldn't escalate through fearing the symptoms and interpreting them as signs of imminent disaster.

Imagine, for example, that you are running for the bus. You might experience the following symptoms:

▶ breathlessness;

▶ pounding heart;

▶ feeling sweaty;

▶ raised blood pressure;

▶ anxiety about missing the bus.

These are some of the same symptoms that you might experience during a panic attack. The difference is that when you are running for the bus, you don't add a second fear to the equation: fear of your symptoms. You might be afraid or worried about missing the bus, but not about the physical and emotional symptoms in your body. You are unlikely to think, 'Goodness, I am breathless, I wonder why? Perhaps there's a problem with my heart?' (unless, of course, you are elderly or have an underlying heart condition). Chances are that you simply think 'I am breathless because I have been running – nothing to be alarmed about.'

Because you can rationalize your symptoms and ascribe a harmless and perfectly acceptable reason for them, they don't worry you. However, when you get the same symptoms during a panic attack, you can't ascribe a rational explanation to them and immediately start to add a second layer of fear – fear of the fear. Because there is no (apparently) reasonable explanation for your symptoms, you assume they are a sign of some imminent catastrophic event – a heart attack, fainting, collapsing, vomiting etc (for more on this, see Chapter 2).

Key idea

Avoid fearing the fear as this will add a second level of anxiety to the experience.

Try it now

What thoughts go through your head when you are having a panic attack? Select from the following common list:

'If I don't get out of here then I am going to...'

* collapse?
* have a heart attack?
* die?
* faint?
* vomit?
* go crazy?
* lose control?
* wet myself?

So, as soon as you experience the symptoms of panic, it is important to remind yourself that they are nothing to fear. This is hard to do. The only way you will learn that the symptoms are harmless, is by experiencing them fully (without escaping to 'safety') – and realizing that you survived! If you keep telling yourself (or accepting) that you are in danger, your body will dutifully react as if you really are in danger and it will produce more symptoms and frighten you more. Sometimes the thoughts are so automatic, or the panic follows them so quickly, that you won't immediately see the connections, but now that you are starting to look for them, you will eventually become more skilled at seeing and interrupting them.

The following are useful self-talk statements to take with you for this stage of the panic attack. Write them out, laminate them and carry them around with you!

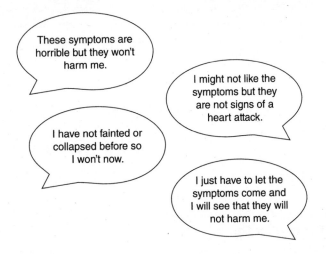

These symptoms are horrible but they won't harm me.

I might not like the symptoms but they are not signs of a heart attack.

I have not fainted or collapsed before so I won't now.

I just have to let the symptoms come and I will see that they will not harm me.

▶ **Step 5: Accept the panic**

Now is the time when you need to learn to accept the panic instead of trying to fight it. Trying to resist the panic, to stop it overwhelming you, is futile, because the more you try to resist it, the more anxious about it you will become – and the more intense the panic will be.

Instead of trying to fight the panic and stop it coming, try to turn the whole situation on its head and start *embracing* the panic; that isn't to say that you will learn to love (or even like) the panic, but that the only way to learn to live with it is to stop being afraid of it – and the only way to stop being afraid of panic attacks is to experience them and learn that you can cope with them.

So, at this stage, you *need* the panic attacks! You need them to come on so that you can practise learning to cope with them! So, stop dreading them and trying to resist them but instead adopt a 'bring it on' attitude!

I hope I have a panic attack so that I can learn how to cope with them.

I am going to relax into the attack and not fight it.

Fighting it is pointless – bring it on!

I know a panic attack won't harm me (though I might not like it!)

Remember this
Fighting the panic will make it worse; the key to success is accepting it.

I often find that when people are given 'permission' to have panic attacks (by being advised to have lots of them), their panic attacks stop.

▶ Step 6: Relax during the panic attack

We have talked earlier (in Step 1) about relaxation tips and how important it is to become generally more relaxed in order to reduce your propensity to getting panic attacks. But, when you are actually in the middle of a panic attack, you need a quick way of being able to relax so that the panic will subside. You cannot have a panic attack and be relaxed – the state of relaxation is incompatible with the highly anxious state of panic.

The first thing to do when you are in the throes of a panic attack, is to slow your breathing down. This is vitally important as it is fast breathing that contributes to many symptoms of panic such as dizziness, chest tightness etc. We breathe fast when we are anxious because our bodies think we are in 'fight or flight' mode and are trying to get as much oxygen into our lungs as possible. This can actually have the opposite effect though: we breathe faster but with shallower breaths which can actually inhibit oxygen flow to the alveoli of the lungs (this is why we feel dizzy).

Key idea

Slowing your breathing down during panic is fundamental to stopping the panic overwhelming you.

So, use your watch to slow your breathing down. The whole breathing in-and-out process should take at least 8–10 seconds. Force yourself to slow your breathing rate down and at the same time, breathe in more deeply.

While you are slowing your breathing rate, draw on the exercises that you learned in Step 1 and say the word 'relax' to yourself each time you breathe out – nice and slowly.

Once you have slowed your breathing rate, do a quick version of the progressive muscle relaxation exercise from Step 1:

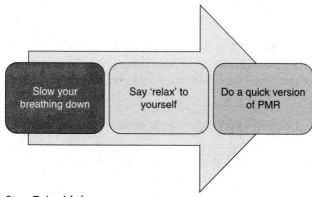

▶ **Step 7: Avoid the escape route**

This step is the most important: do not escape! Escape is what you have been doing before but, of course, running away only reinforces the link between avoidance and relief. Running away reinforces the view in your brain that there is something genuinely dangerous about the situation you are facing, or about your symptoms, or about the way that you feel. It might provide immediate relief but escaping makes things worse in the long run.

Each time you face your fears and accept your feelings is a step forward. Each time you escape or avoid is a lost opportunity to take a step forward. The graphs overleaf (reproduced from Chapter 4) illustrate vividly what happens to your anxiety levels if you keep escaping – and what happens to them if you stay put. They show that the anxiety eventually subsides if you stay with it, as the human body cannot maintain the very high level of arousal required in a panic attack.

If you escape, the panic will keep returning:

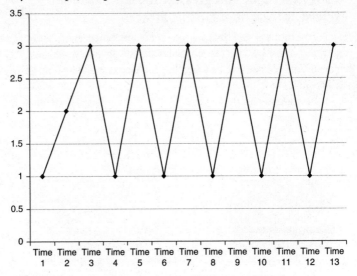

If you stay, the panic will eventually subside on its own:

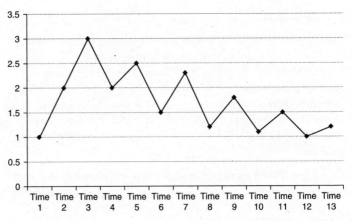

It is worth noting here that the panic will always subside, even if you don't do anything to help it. In other words, even if you don't actually follow Steps 1–6 and go straight to Step 7, the panic will still subside! But Steps 1–6 are designed to help you cope with the panic attack and make things much easier for you – most people would be unlikely to be able to go straight to Step 7 without going through the other steps in the process.

Key idea

If you stay exposed to the source of your fear, the panic will eventually subside on its own.

PROBLEMS YOU MAY HAVE WITH THE PROGRAMME

It is entirely possible that you will encounter difficulties with any step of the programme. Some of the more common difficulties are outlined below:

▶ **Difficulties in relaxing (Steps 1 and 6).** Sometimes people experience cramp or pain while attempting the progressive muscle exercises. This can be frightening but it is not dangerous. If you get cramp don't abandon the exercises, just rub the affected muscle and try again but more gently. Or, leave the muscle to recover while you move on to other muscle groups.

▶ **Inability to control thoughts (in all the steps).** Most thoughts associated with panic and anxiety are automatic and it is, indeed, very difficult to control them. It is quite normal to have difficulty with intruding or unhelpful thoughts that seem to 'get in the way' of your progress. Try not to dwell on them or worry about them – accept that they will drift into your mind from time to time. And remember, practice is the key to success and it will not happen overnight.

▶ **Trying too hard.** Sometimes you can try too hard and spend all your time worrying about whether the programme is 'working'. This has the effect of swapping one set of anxieties for another and is counter-productive. Try not to be preoccupied with thoughts of 'Am I relaxed? Am I still panicking? Is it working?', just let whatever sensations of relaxation appear and wash over you, without worrying about whether they are 'enough'.

Coping with nocturnal panic attacks

Nocturnal panic attacks, or panic attacks that wake you up in the night, are surprisingly common. Because they wake you and disrupt your sleep, you become chronically tired – and anxious about your inability to get a good night's sleep. This leads to a vicious cycle – the more anxious you are, the less likely you are to sleep well and the more likely you are to have nocturnal panic episodes (see diagram below).

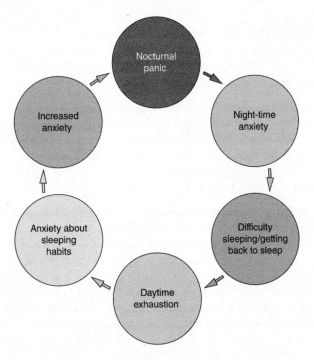

Cope with nocturnal panic then, using the following steps:

▶ When you go to bed, stop dreading the panic attack! Instead, use *paradoxical intention* to actually try to induce an attack; tell yourself that you want and need an attack in order to practise your new coping skills.

▶ If you get an attack, reassure yourself that it won't harm you and is not a sign of imminent disaster.

▶ If you are unable to go back to sleep, get up for a bit, read, watch TV etc. Don't worry about not being able to fall asleep! The only thing stopping you from sleeping is the anxiety about not sleeping! The golden rule to remember is:

▷ If you are tired enough and relaxed enough, you will sleep.

▷ Conversely, you will not sleep if you are either not tired enough, or not relaxed enough.

Mythbuster

Being tired is not enough to get you to sleep, you need to be relaxed too.

▶ Use the progressive muscle relaxation technique in Chapter 3 to help you to relax and fall asleep – but don't worry if they do not appear to be 'working'.

▶ During the day, don't get anxious about your lack of sleep. Use your exhaustion as a way of proving to yourself how you can cope with very little sleep – this will reduce your anxiety about being unable to cope (see Charlotte's case study below).

▶ Don't sleep during the day, do exercise instead. Remember that in order to sleep well, you need to be both tired and relaxed. Engaging in excessive exercise will help!

▶ Don't spend the day worrying about your inability to sleep. Remind yourself that you can cope with little sleep (although it will feel horrible) and that it is only your anxiety about not sleeping that is keeping you awake.

Mythbuster

Sometimes people think they are so tired that they should 'catch up' on lost sleep during the day – this is likely to exacerbate night-time sleeping difficulties.

Case study

Charlotte had suffered from panic attacks and severe anxiety for over a year. She recently started to develop nocturnal panic attacks too and it was at this point that she presented at my clinic. She felt she could just about manage her daytime attacks, but now that she was getting them at night too, she felt she couldn't cope. She would wake up in the middle of the night in absolute terror and drenched in sweat – her heart would be pounding, and she would be struggling to breathe. Sometimes she felt like she was choking too. These feelings would absolutely terrify her and she felt that she would surely die. It would take a long time to calm down and she was invariably unable to get back to sleep. In fact, it was getting to the stage where she was afraid to even go to sleep in the first place in case she woke up with a panic attack. Obviously, her sleep was becoming severely disrupted and she was exhausted during the day and felt she could not function. She felt it was unsafe to drive when she was so tired and she couldn't work or even shop due to her exhaustion. She would drink lots of caffeine to cope during the day but spend most of her time worrying about how tired she was, how she would manage and what would become of her if she didn't get a decent night's sleep.

Her general anxiety levels during the day also meant that she was getting ever more daytime panic attacks too, to the extent that she spent most of the day in bed, unable and too afraid to get up except to meet the most basic of functions.

When she came to the clinic we agreed on a programme of action. This involved learning and practising progressive muscle relaxation techniques, and learning how to cope with the daytime panic. Charlotte was advised to get up during the day and take long walks and try to function normally – to prove to herself that she could. She stopped all the caffeine intake. She learned that she could function even when severely sleep-deprived, although it was very unpleasant to do so. But realizing that she could cope helped her relax a little bit about the lack of sleep. She learned to stop worrying about sleeping and that she had to be both relaxed and tired for sleep to come. This helped her get to sleep at night and also helped her to cope when she had panic attacks. But, once she stopped fearing the attacks, they became less frequent and thus she slept better. Lowering her general anxiety during the day helped to reduce her daytime panic attacks too.

Panic attacks and 'stage fright'

Performance anxiety is the term used for people who have severe anxiety about performing – such as in sport, music or public speaking. Stage fright can even occur during written exams. While many professional performers use propranolol (beta blockers) to reduce anxiety. One study (Tindall, 2004) suggested that around a quarter of professional musicians use the drug. Stage fright, however, is the same as any other panic attack and can be treated with the same techniques as described in this chapter. Here are some extra tips to help you overcome panic associated with performance-based situations:

AHEAD OF THE EVENT

▶ Visualize yourself performing while conducting the progressive muscle relaxation technique; go through your entire performance in your head.

▶ Prepare 'self-talk' messages such as: 'I have done this before and was fine – there is no reason why I shouldn't be now'.

▶ Reduce the importance you are placing on your success at the performance: panic comes when we think that a successful performance is absolutely essential. Thus, exams or auditions can appear to affect your entire life and take on life-or-death properties; try to gain perspective – you won't die or get hurt if you make a mistake. Read some true-life stories of people suffering illness or tragedy – this can help put your worry of performance failure into the perspective you need.

▶ Performance anxiety emanates from 'musts' and 'awfuls': 'I must do well; it will be awful if I don't'. Eliminate these! By indulging in musts and awfuls (or exaggerated catastrophizing) you are in danger of creating a self-fulfilling prophecy.

JUST BEFORE THE EVENT

▶ Practise your relaxation techniques before your performance. Go through each muscle in turn while you are waiting to begin.

DURING THE EVENT

▶ If you feel anxious or that panic is coming, make sure you slow your breathing down and start the progressive muscle tensing and relaxing. No one will be able to see you do this.

▶ Buy yourself recovery time by having a bottle of water handy and slowly drinking from it (where possible).

▶ Remind yourself that you are perfectly capable – the only thing you are fearing is fear itself.

▶ Reduce your need for approval; part of the anxiety of stage fright stems from the desire to be liked/approved of/well thought of by your audience. Reduce your reliance on this approval by reminding yourself that you are doing this for your own enjoyment as much as theirs!

▶ Accept mistakes; you don't have to be perfect. To err, as they say, is human.

▶ Act like you are confident – this can 'trick' your brain (and your audience) into believing in you.

▶ Try to enjoy what you are doing – have fun with it!

In general, applying the same principles to stage fright as to any other panic attack situation, means that the more you are exposed to your feared situation, the less panicky you will become. This means that you should practise performing as much as possible – take any opportunity to perform, rather than trying to avoid it.

Case study

Jed, at 25, had never experienced panic attacks or anxiety before. He had a good job as an advertising executive, which involved giving presentations or 'pitches' to clients. He enjoyed his job, but one day, he was in the middle of a presentation in front of several colleagues and several members of the client organization. He was suddenly overwhelmed by panic – his heart started pumping, he started sweating profusely, he felt a wave of heat overtake him and experienced an impending sense of doom. He did not know what was happening to him and felt that he was surely going to have a heart attack or collapse. His colleagues noticed that he suddenly looked unwell and asked if he was OK. He replied that he felt a bit faint and they suggested a break during which drinks of water were fetched and Jed went to get some fresh air.

He felt better but was puzzled about what had happened. Someone else took over his presentation and the next morning he visited his doctor for a check-up. All was fine and the doctor said he had had a panic attack. Jed was relieved that there was nothing serious and got on with his life. The problem came the next time he was expected to give a presentation. He started to worry beforehand that he would have another attack. He also worried about how he would come across – whether his presentation would be acceptable. What would happen if he forgot what he was going to say or made a stupid comment? Or if his mind went blank? Or maybe he would be asked a difficult question – Jed became very anxious and when it came to the time to speak, he experienced another panic attack. This time, he was too embarrassed to leave the room and so tried to get through the presentation as best he could. However, his boss commented later that the presentation didn't go well. This made Jed even more anxious, and it got to the stage where he simply felt unable to stand up in front of people and give a presentation. He started making excuses to avoid them. The panicky feelings even spread to meetings in case he was expected to speak in front of people.

Things got so bad that he even considered leaving his job and looking for a new career – one which didn't involve any form of public speaking.

Focus points

✳ Becoming generally more relaxed is the first step to reducing the likelihood of experiencing on-going panic attacks. This can be achieved through relaxation techniques and thought-challenging.

✳ The trick to beating panic is to search out situations that might induce panic rather than trying to avoid them. The more you experience the panic, the more you can learn to cope with it.

✳ Night-time panic attacks can disrupt your sleeping patterns and create a vicious cycle of anxiety, sleep deprivation and panic. Break the cycle at various points by learning to accept the panic and its impact.

✳ Panic attacks can lead to performance anxiety but this should be treated in the same way as any other panic-inducing situation, e.g. with graded exposure and relaxation.

✳ Don't worry if you have setbacks; these are inevitable but a bad panic attack won't undo all your hard work. You should find that setbacks are fairly easy to cope with if you don't get too wound up about them.

6

Complex phobias

In this chapter you will learn:

▶ *About complex phobias*
▶ *How to deal with agoraphobia*
▶ *How to deal with social phobia*

How do you feel?

1 Do you avoid going to places where there is no easy means of escape?   Yes/No

2 Does worry about what other people might think of you stop you going to certain places?   Yes/No

3 Do you get very anxious in social situations?   Yes/No

4 Do crowded places cause you severe anxiety?   Yes/No

5 Does speaking in public or in a group cause you severe anxiety? Yes/No

Whereas specific phobias are anxieties about a particular situation or object (see Chapter 7), complex phobias can involve several anxieties or sources of fear. The most common complex phobias are agoraphobia and social phobia. If you ticked 'yes' to any of the above, this chapter is for you.

Agoraphobia

Agoraphobia is often thought of as a fear of 'open spaces' but this is a rather simplistic view; agoraphobia is more likely to be characterized by a fear of public spaces or crowds and can thus involve fear of travelling on public transport or even entering shops. Agoraphobia is usually intimately linked with panic attacks and sufferers often fear the consequences of having a panic attack in a public place. The DSM-IV defines agoraphobia as:

> 'The presence of anxiety in situations or places in which individuals fear being embarrassed, or being unable to escape or get help if a panic attack occurs.'

These feared situations tend to be avoided or, if they can't be avoided, approached with a great deal of anxiety and distress. Agoraphobia tends to appear between the ages of 15 and 35, with the most common times of onset being either late adolescence or around 30 years of age (Perugi, Frare and Toni, 2007). Women are more likely than men to suffer from agoraphobia and it is rare to develop the condition after the mid-forties. Often a panic attack comes 'out of the blue' in a public place and this leads to avoidance and fears of repeated attacks which, over time, can lead to full-blown agoraphobia (see Figure 6.1, repeated from

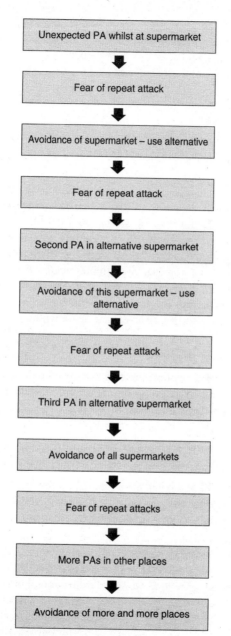

Figure 6.1 How avoidance and fear can lead to agoraphobia

Chapter 2). This avoidance can have a serious impact on everyday life as sufferers become increasingly limited to where they can go and what they can do; shopping, socializing and work may become impossible and the sufferer can become housebound.

Mythbuster

Agoraphobia is not something that only older people get – in fact, it is surprisingly common among adolescents.

Many sufferers hide or cope with their condition for years, by adapting their lives in ways that minimize contact with their feared situation; in today's internet world, this is easier to achieve than previously, as people can now shop on the internet, have a social life via social networking sites (e.g. Facebook) and perhaps even work from home using computer-mediated communication. They may only seek help when their circumstances change, e.g. they lose or change their job or suffer a bereavement, forcing them to face their fears and engage again with the outside world.

Remember this

The internet and social networking availability today mean that people with agoraphobia can manage their lives without ever facing their fears – which means they are less likely to seek help.

It is, perhaps, unsurprising that sufferers may develop secondary conditions too, such as social anxiety, depression or hypochondria.

Agoraphobia nearly always occurs alongside panic attacks, usually because the agoraphobia has developed as a result of PA (due to avoidance of situations where escape seems difficult).

THE ROLE OF PERFECTIONISM

Perfectionism is thought to play a role in the development and maintenance of a range of anxiety disorders. For example, within obsessive–compulsive disorder (see Chapter 9) it is thought that some obsessions (such as doubts that actions have been performed correctly) and compulsive actions (e.g. washing hands until it feels 'right') might be partly attributable to perfectionist thinking (Iketani, et al, 2002). Social phobia (see below), by definition, involves a preoccupation with one's social performance and doubts about effectiveness.

A study in 2002 suggested that perfectionism may also be related to the development and maintenance of agoraphobia, in that such sufferers might have a tendency to set excessively high standards for themselves which leads to undue self-criticism (Iketani, et al, 2002).

Case study

Sara had always been a perfectionist who always felt that it was important to get things right. She worked hard at school and was always concerned about her appearance – she was the sort of child who hated getting messy. As an adult, she had the same level of perfectionism when it came to her social life, and she would plan 'perfect' dinner parties and nights out. Her problems began years ago when she went to university; not only was she meeting a lot of new people at the same time, but she felt that her high standards were not met by the other people around her. Indeed, people would tease her for keeping her flat clean and tidy and for being so organized. She began to feel out of control because the other students she shared with were messy – they left crockery in the sink and old food in the fridge etc.

She also began to feel awkward when talking to them. She felt that she had little in common with them and started to stutter and feel uncomfortable when interacting with them. She thought they were laughing at her behind her back. Her anxiety about her situation grew and she had her first panic attack when a group of students were talking to her in the canteen; she remembers feeling that they were almost interviewing her and treating her like an oddity. She became flustered and panicky, and after that she started to avoid going to the canteen.

However, her anxiety grew, and she began to dislike talking to any students. She started to keep herself to herself more and tried to avoid talking to anyone else. She stayed in her room more and more. When she went to lectures, she kept her head down and let her hair hang loose so it covered her face. If she was required to speak to anyone, she avoided eye contact and kept her voice low, in the hope that the interaction would end before she had a panic attack.

She got through her university years but remained fearful of crowds, of talking to people and of going out, especially when there was little means for escape. She worried about embarrassing herself by having an obvious panic attack, or about being laughed at. She found a job in a small office where there were only a couple other workers so she managed to cope. She started to do her shopping online so she could cut down on the likelihood of having to talk to strangers.

She realized she needed help though; she was desperate to be able to live a normal life and go out occasionally – and even meet a man and settle down and have a family. She came to my clinic where it became apparent that she was suffering from agoraphobia, but with elements of social phobia too.

DEALING WITH AGORAPHOBIA

Because agoraphobia is so closely related to panic attack disorder, there are two approaches to learning how to manage it: one is based on the phobia itself, and the other is based on dealing with panic attacks. Dealing with panic attacks is covered in Chapter 5, so won't be repeated here; instead we will focus on developing a specific programme for managing agoraphobia. This is based on the material presented in Chapter 4 so it would be useful to revisit that chapter first.

PROGRAMME FOR COPING WITH AGORAPHOBIA

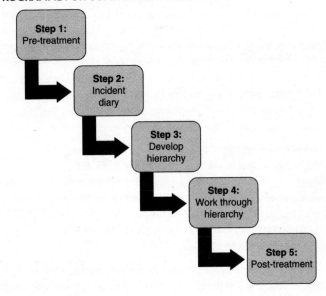

Step 1:
Pre-treatment

Step 2:
Incident diary

Step 3:
Develop hierarchy

Step 4:
Work through hierarchy

Step 5:
Post-treatment

▶ Step 1: How severe is your phobia?

Start by obtaining a measure of how agoraphobic you are – or how severe your symptoms are. This can be used as a way of charting your progress (in conjunction with the hierarchy in Step 3 below). Your agoraphobic severity is affected by two factors – how much you avoid situations and how anxious they make you feel. The following questionnaire will help you work out your pre-treatment score.

Remember this

Agoraphobia severity is affected by how much you avoid situations and by how anxious they make you feel.

Severity of agoraphobia questionnaire
Score each of the following situations in terms of how much you currently avoid it and how anxious it makes you feel. Score 1–5 using the following scales:

1 No anxiety	2 Some anxiety	3 Moderate anxiety	5 Quite a lot of anxiety	5 A great deal of anxiety
1 Do not avoid	2 Sometimes avoid	3 Often avoid	4 Usually avoid	5 Always avoid

Situation	Anxiety score	Avoidance score
Leaving my house alone		
Walking down a busy street		
Walking down a quiet street		
Going into a busy shop		
Speaking to a shop assistant		
Eating in a restaurant		
Going on a bus unaccompanied		
Being in a crowded place		
Driving my car alone		
Going to a cinema		

Continued

Situation	Anxiety score	Avoidance score
Attending a work meeting		
Going to an unfamiliar place		
Going somewhere with no easy exit		
Speaking in front of people		
Going to places where there are a lot of people my own age		
Going to places where there are people I know		
Going to places where there are strangers		
Going somewhere where people will notice if I have a panic attack		

We will return to this questionnaire later on; it will be useful to chart your progress.

▶ Step 2: Keep a diary

Keep an incident diary, noting what you were doing before the incident, how you felt, what you did and also rating your level of anxiety. This will be needed for Step 3 (developing a personal hierarchy). An 'incident' in your diary is any one of the following:

▶ Anything that happens which makes you feel uncomfortable or gives you a panic attack.

▶ Anything that could be classed as avoidance – e.g. taking a different route to get somewhere, or setting off somewhere but changing your mind so that you don't have to go.

▶ Incidents could also include places that would normally induce anxiety but which you have managed to get to with little anxiety; at this stage, these incidents are likely to be few and far between, but you never know!

the following for your incident diary

e	What were you doing before the incident? (e.g. walking, having an argument, driving somewhere etc.)	What happened?	How did you feel?	What did you do? (e.g. escaped, stayed etc.)	What was your anxiety level on a scale of 0–100 (100 being the most anxious you have ever felt)?

You should keep this diary for at least a week, ideally for a month. Only go on to Step 3 when you have sufficient diary entries to work with.

Situational hierarchy

Step	Task or situation
1	
2	
3	
4	
5	
6	
7	
8	
9	
10	

▶ Step 3: Create your situational hierarchy

Now that you have completed Steps 1 and 2, it should be easier for you to identify your challenges and put them into an order of difficulty (fill in the grid opposite). For example, in Step 1, you have scores for those situations that you find most anxiety-provoking, but it is only by cross-checking these against the diaries in Step 2, that you will be better able to gauge their accuracy (or to see if any situations relevant to you are missing from that questionnaire).

Your personal hierarchy should start with those situations which you find slightly challenging, but that you can achieve. They should build in difficulty so that, as you get near the top of your hierarchy, or ladder, there will be situations there which you simply cannot imagine ever being able to achieve!

Key idea

Developing a situational hierarchy in order to carry out graded exposure is an essential stage in the treatment of agoraphobia.

You may have more than 10 items in your hierarchy of course – some people have 20 or more!

▶ Step 4: Use your situational hierarchy

Now you will need to start working your way up through your hierarchy. In order to do this, you will need to revisit the material from Chapter 4 and Chapter 5, in particular: challenging negative thoughts, relaxation and developing distractors (Chapter 4) and dealing with anticipation, dealing with the fear of the fear, accepting the panic and avoiding the escape route (Chapter 5). It is useful to keep a diary of your progress which should include the following sections for each step in the hierarchy:

Hierarchy Step 1: ....

Date of attempt	Anxiety levels 0–100 before, during and after	Any negative thoughts?	Challenges to negative thoughts	Outcome

ate of ttempt	Anxiety levels 0–100 before, during and after	Any negative thoughts?	Challenges to negative thoughts	Outcome

Each step should continue until little or no anxiety is felt and the step is easily achievable.

Remember this

Don't start the next step in the hierarchy until you have really mastered the previous one – this means that you can perform the behaviour with no anxiety at all.

▶ Step 5: Check your progress

Now repeat Step 1 (reproduced below) in order to see how much you have improved!

Severity of agoraphobia questionnaire (post-treatment)
Score each of the following situations in terms of how much you currently avoid it and how anxious it makes you feel. Score 1–5 using the following scales:

1 No anxiety	2 Some anxiety	3 Moderate anxiety	5 Quite a lot of anxiety	5 A great deal of anxiety
1 Do not avoid	2 Sometimes avoid	3 Often avoid	4 Usually avoid	5 Always avoid

Situation	Anxiety score	Avoidance score
Leaving my house alone		
Walking down a busy street		
Walking down a quiet street		
Going into a busy shop		
Speaking to a shop assistant		
Eating in a restaurant		
Going on a bus unaccompanied		
Being in a crowded place		
Driving my car alone		
Going to a cinema		
Attending a work meeting		
Going to an unfamiliar place		
Going somewhere with no easy exit		
Speaking in front of people		
Going to places where there are a lot of people my own age		

Situation	Anxiety score	Avoidance score
Going to places where there are people I know		
Going to places where there are strangers		
Going somewhere where people will notice if I have a panic attack		

Social phobia

Social phobia is sometimes known as social anxiety disorder. Humans are inherently social beings and good social relationships can offer important social support and contribute to one's sense of well-being. Yet people with social phobia fear and avoid engaging with other people in social interactions, often because of a marked fear that they will be judged unfavourably and suffer social rejection.

According to the DSM-IV, social phobia is characterized by:

> 'A marked or persistent fear of social or performance situations in which embarrassment may occur, leading to marked distress…that can severely interfere with his or her work, education or social activities.'

It is thought that around 7 to 13 per cent of the population will experience social phobia at some point in their lives (Pet, et al, 2010) and it typically develops in adolescence (often among young people who were shy or anxious children). The numbers of sufferers are higher in college populations than in the general population, which might be because this is the stage in life when people typically encounter a lot of new people and new situations, at a time when social acceptance may be particularly important. The condition is characterized by an excessive fear of social evaluation – in other words, a strong fear of what others may think of the sufferer. Students tend to be facing new situations and people without the support of the familiar family and friends that they have grown up with.

It is thought to be the third most common mental disorder in adults worldwide and women are slightly more likely to suffer from it than men (Veale, 2003).

Interestingly, it is thought that fewer than ten per cent of sufferers seek professional input for social phobia (Pet, et al, 2010), with many suffering for more than 15 years before seeking help. This might be because they don't know where to go for help or are too embarrassed to seek help. Even when they do access treatment, it is often someone else who initiates it on their behalf (e.g. a family member or friend).

Like other complex phobias, sufferers of Social Phobia tend to be at higher risk of developing other psychiatric conditions, in particular depression (see Chapter 10 for more on depression). Research has also shown that sufferers tend to have more alcohol dependence than other populations (Pet, et al, 2010), and this could be because alcohol might be used as a crutch for people who find social situations difficult.

CHARACTERISTICS OF SOCIAL PHOBIA

The core element then of social phobia is *the fear of negative evaluation by others*. Social phobia thus leads to avoidance of those situations where such evaluation is likely. These can typically include:

- public speaking;
- talking to a group or in a meeting;
- parties;
- eating/drinking in public;
- speaking to a stranger;
- dating.

Social phobics tend to have high standards or rules (see section on perfectionism, earlier in this chapter) about how they should perform in social situations. If they fail to achieve these standards, they feel that others might judge them as inferior or inadequate (an assessment with which they agree). They also feel that this negative evaluation by others will lead to catastrophic circumstances such as social rejection ('no one will ever like me') or failure to achieve a goal ('I will never get a job').

The typical negative evaluations that are feared tend to include;

▶ that their hands might shake or tremble and be noticed;

▶ that their palms might be sweaty when shaking hands;

▶ that they might say something 'stupid';

▶ that they might do something stupid (e.g. trip);

▶ that they might look stupid or odd.

> **Remember this**
>
> The key factor of social phobia is the fear of negative evaluation by other people.

Social phobia has a number of characteristics:

▶ Groups tend to provoke more anxiety than individuals.

▶ Same-age peers tend to provoke more anxiety that older (or younger) individuals.

▶ People of the opposite gender usually provoke more anxiety than those of the same gender.

▶ Authority figures usually provoke more anxiety than people of equal standing.

▶ Sufferers often feel a range of emotions such as anxiety, shame and even self-disgust or anger (Veale, 2003).

There are two main types of social phobia: generalized and non-generalized.

Generalized social phobia: this tends to be more disabling because there is a range of quite diverse situations that cause the extreme anxiety (and avoidance).

Non-generalized social phobia: this tends to be associated with a more limited range of situations (such as public speaking). Anxiety about performing sexually, or even urinating in public toilets when others are in earshot, can be part of this syndrome.

HOW DOES SOCIAL PHOBIA DEVELOP?

It is thought that socially anxious people are hyper-vigilant when detecting stimuli in the environment that might be a social threat to them. This means that they might be very sensitive to other people appearing to laugh at them, criticize them, disparage them or threaten their self-esteem in any way. Such people may pay particular attention to 'social threat' cues indicating disapproval from others (such as expressions of anger or disgust) and may even look out for and anticipate such cues. This is termed *selective attention* by psychologists because it means that such people selectively attend to those things which could be perceived as negative, while paying less attention to those which could be perceived as positive.

Remember this

People with social phobia seem to pay more attention to cues that might indicate negative evaluation – and to misread neutral cues in a negative way.

Some researchers suggest it is not only that socially anxious people notice 'social threat' cues more than non-anxious people, but that socially anxious people also have particular difficulties in disengaging from these cues – e.g. they find it hard to stop thinking about the possible threat they have observed. They may also have a processing problem that leads them to incorrectly evaluating social cues – for example, having a bias towards 'confirmatory' information which seeks to confirm their suspicions that other people dislike them. This helps create a mindset of '*maladaptive beliefs*' about their own social performance; in other words, because they attend so much to the negative feedback that they think they can perceive, they believe they are doing less well in a social setting than they actually are.

Thus, it is proposed that there a number of processes which can lead to social phobia:

▶ **Hyper-vigilance:** people scrutinize their environment and themselves for possible signs of danger – such signs could include a frown from someone they are speaking to, or the feeling of blushing in themselves.

▶ **Avoidance:** they start to avoid paying attention to some aspects of the social interaction so as to avoid seeing threatening stimuli – for example they might avoid eye contact or avoid looking at themselves in the mirror. They might also escape from or avoid the social situation altogether which helps perpetuate the problem, as they can never learn that their fears might be unjustified.

▶ **Heightened sense of self:** they become excessively self-focused as they are preoccupied with how others might see them.

▶ **Inadequate processing:** sufferers do not adequately process any information that may contradict their negative beliefs about their social world.

▶ **Attention to flaws:** they become more and more aware of the flaws in their social performance.

▶ **Self-fulfilling prophecy:** these processes may make the person more anxious and the symptoms of anxiety themselves may interfere with their social functioning – which goes to confirm their own negative beliefs about themselves (i.e. their beliefs become a self-fulfilling prophecy).

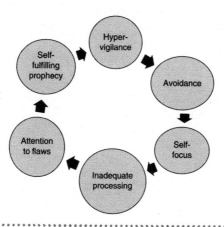

Key idea

Becoming less vigilant to 'threat' and less self-focused on your own performance can help in overcoming social phobia.

Mythbuster

It should be noted that people with social phobia don't necessarily lack social skills. In most cases, these people have perfectly good social skills and can interact normally with people they feel comfortable with (e.g. their partner, close friends and family members). People who lack social skills even in these familiar situations have a different problem (for example, people with Asperger's Syndrome). However, in situations where sufferers feel uncomfortable, their anxiety can make them appear socially inept (as explained above) as they undertake a range of adaptive behaviours:

- They might try too hard to be amusing.

- They might avoid eye contact.

- They might interact less.

- They might keep their head lowered.

- They might refuse to reveal personal information.

- They might reveal too much information out of nerves.

All this, of course, leads to the self-fulfilling prophecy as outlined above. Some of these are actually *safety mechanisms* in that the individual tries to take the action in an attempt to prevent the feared catastrophe (or rejection) occurring – e.g. someone who fears that they may visibly sweat under their arms may press their arms close to their body, but this can increase the sweating. But these safety behaviours can make things worse (self-fulfilling prophecy) because they help the sufferer to focus too much on themselves to determine if the action is 'working', or they may even make the symptoms that they fear worse. Safety behaviours can also draw attention to the feared symptoms (e.g. if they worry about people seeing them blush and thus keep their head lowered, this is likely to lead others to focus on them even more as they appear 'odd').

Case study

Emily had always been a very anxious person, especially in social situations. She describes herself as having been a shy child who found it hard to make friends. She reports that she was bullied for many years at school, because she was different from her peers, and she became quite socially isolated. As an adolescent, her social anxieties became so severe that she felt unable to go into any social situation without experiencing a great deal of anxiety and even panic. She presented with a range of social-phobia type issues.

Emily kept diaries to record her thoughts and feelings in social situations. I was also able to observe her in some situations with strangers to see if her perceptions about her performance were the same as the reality. It transpired that Emily would become extremely wary in social situations and would spend a lot of time observing other people around her. In order to do this 'in peace', she would try to make herself as invisible as possible – by slumping, lowering her head etc. She also tended to seize upon any possible hint of social rejection as a way of 'proving' her own theories (that no one liked her). For example, in one case, she went up to a food counter to order a coffee. I was observing her. The assistant took her order but in the middle of doing so, addressed a comment to his colleague. Later, Emily interpreted this as a negative comment about her, even though she couldn't hear what was being said. I suggested that there might be alternative explanations (e.g. the assistant could have been asking for change or help etc.) which she eventually accepted.

I also noticed that Emily behaved in a way that discouraged people from interacting with her: she avoided eye contact, mumbled and looked uncomfortable. The reactions of people added 'evidence' to Emily that she was socially inept. However, when I observed her, I noticed positive reactions too, such as someone smiling at her; interestingly, Emily did not notice this at all, preferring to focus instead on her 'failures'.

HOW DOES SOCIAL PHOBIA DIFFER FROM SHYNESS?

It has been suggested by some that social phobia is just extreme shyness – and even that the medical professional is responsible for labelling a normal human condition as a 'phobia' in order to boost pharmaceutical sales of anti-anxiety drugs. However, one study that examined this proposition found that although 62 per cent of parents labelled their adolescent children as shy, fewer than 9 per cent of them met DSM-IV criteria for social phobia. The authors of this study thus concluded that social phobia is not simply shyness (Burstein, Ameli-Grillon and Merikangas, 2011).

There are also other common conditions that can be confused with social phobia which include the following:

▶ **Body dysmorphia:** here sufferers believe that their appearance is a problem (e.g. they believe they are too fat or ugly) but they may be unwilling to reveal (to other people) this preoccupation with their appearance and thus tend to present with symptoms more common to social anxiety. They prefer others to think they have social anxiety rather than draw further attention to their body by explaining the real source of their angst.

▶ **Olfactory reference syndrome:** here sufferers believe that they have an unpleasant body odour, which they go to great lengths to mask with perfumes, fragrances or by avoiding social interactions.

It is thus important when treating social phobia to be sure that this is what it actually is.

Mythbuster

Social phobia is not the same as extreme shyness.

PROGRAMME FOR COPING WITH SOCIAL PHOBIA

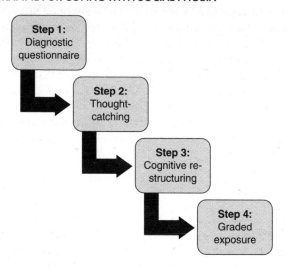

Step 1:
Diagnostic
questionnaire

Step 2:
Thought-
catching

Step 3:
Cognitive re-
structuring

Step 4:
Graded
exposure

▷ Step 1: Determine the nature and severity of your phobia

The first stage of a treatment programme is to determine a) if you actually do have social phobia (rather than a related condition) and b) whether it is severe or debilitating enough to require input. Use the following questionnaire as a starting point:

w difficult do you find the following situations?

	1 Fairly easy	2 Makes me anxious	3 Makes me very anxious	4 Makes me extremely anxious but I don't avoid doing it	5 I avoid this where possible
blic speaking (e.g. giving resentation)					
lking to a group or in a eeting					
tending a party					
ting/drinking in public					

Continued

	1 Fairly easy	2 Makes me anxious	3 Makes me very anxious	4 Makes me extremely anxious but I don't avoid doing it	5 I avoid this where possibl
Speaking to a stranger (e.g. in a shop)					
Participating in activities in which I am the centre of attention					
Speaking to other people my own age					
Speaking to people in authority					
Being in situations in which I might blush					
Being in situations in which I might be judged					
Being in situations in which I might get embarrassed					
Being in situations where people might see me trembling or shaking					
Being in situations where I might do something stupid					

	1 Fairly easy	2 Makes me anxious	3 Makes me very anxious	4 Makes me extremely anxious but I don't avoid doing it	5 I avoid this where possible
...ing in situations where ...ight say something ...pid					
...eting new people					
...aking a complaint					
...ing complimented					
...expectedly bumping ...o someone I know					

Scores of 3 or more for more than three items suggest some form of social phobia. The closer the overall score is to 90, the more intense the social phobia is likely to be. All this assumes that:

▶ You have no difficulty interacting with close friends and family.

▶ You are not overly convinced that your social difficulties are entirely due to your appearance (though it is common for people to lack confidence in their appearance).

▶ Your social difficulties are not due to a belief that you have an unpleasant body odour.

▶ Step 2: Catch your thoughts and emotions

In order to get a better picture of not just what situations cause you difficulty, but what thoughts and emotions are associated with them, it is worth keeping a diary, using the template below.

Incident that caused difficulty	What thoughts went through your head?	What emotions did you feel?
	e.g. I bet I look really stupid I am going to say something daft Everyone is looking at me	e.g. embarrassed, ashamed

▶ Step 3: Cognitive restructuring

This is where you start to correct negative or inaccurate thoughts that you 'caught' in your diary in Step 2. This is based on the assumption that (a) your beliefs about the dangers or threats imposed by social situations are incorrect, (b) that you might have flawed predictions about the outcomes of these situations and that (c) you probably have inaccurate, biased processing while in the social situation.

Key idea

Replacing thinking errors with more helpful thoughts is a vital step in treating social phobia.

Go back through your diary and identify examples of where you have demonstrated any of the cognitive distortions outlined in Chapter 3. They are listed here as a reminder, with examples relating to social phobia (and some additional ones particularly relevant to social phobia):

Cognitive distortions or unhelpful patterns of thinking (sometimes called thinking errors), based on Burns (1989)

All-or-nothing thinking	Things are either good or bad e.g. 'I won't have anyone to talk to at the party' or 'I will give a bad presentation'.
Mental filter/ discounting the positive	Only noticing and paying attention to the negatives (e.g. the one person who ignored you or the one mistake you made) while ignoring the positives (e.g. the people who smiled at you or the laughs you got at the appropriate point during your presentation).
Over-generalization	When something negative happens, you generalize it e.g. 'I stumbled over my words – I always speak badly in public'.
Mind-reading	Assuming that you know what others are thinking e.g. 'They think I am really stupid'.
Fortune-telling	Predicting how things will turn out: 'No one will talk to me at the party'.
Magnification/ catastrophizing	Blowing things out of proportion so that they take on catastrophic qualities: e.g. 'I did poorly in the presentation – I will never be asked to do one again and I will lose my job'.
Emotional reasoning	Reasoning from your emotions: you feel stupid so assume that you are stupid.
Should-ing	Being preoccupied with what you 'should have' done in a social situation e.g. you 'should' have made a witty comment.
Labelling	Giving yourself a negative label based on one thing you may have done: I said something stupid, therefore I am an idiot.
Self-blame	Taking the blame and responsibility for too much; e.g. 'That person yawned while we were talking; I must have bored her'.

There are also some thinking errors specific to social phobia

High personal standards	Expecting every social interaction to be perfect and that you must be – for example – witty or intelligent, even if other people are not so perfect all the time. Challenge this by looking for evidence that others make mistakes too but are not socially rejected.
Assumption of negative evaluation	Social phobics assume others are judging them unfavourably so challenge this by asking these questions: What evidence is there that they are judging me? Why do I care if they are judging me? What effect would their judgements of me have in the long term?

Identify the thinking errors you have made in your diaries, write them out in the following template and suggest alternative explanations in the next column (e.g. 'She may have yawned because she was tired, not because I was boring her'). You should also read Chapter 10 which deals with self-esteem, as negative self-esteem issues are often tied in with social phobia.

Thinking errors identified	Alternative explanations

▶ Step 4: Graded exposure

This is where a situational hierarchy is constructed in exactly the same way as for any phobia (see Chapter 4 and the section on agoraphobia above). A detailed hierarchy is made of all the situations that you fear or avoid, and they are rated in order to create a 'ladder' with the easiest items at the lowest rungs and the more difficult situations at the top of the ladder. Self-exposure means that you repeatedly face the feared situations in a gradual manner until the anxiety is reduced to such a level that the situation is easily manageable.

Sample situational hierarchy for social phobia

NB: Everyone's hierarchy will look different, but this is a sample to show you how one might look.

Step	Task or situation
1	Walk past a group of people of similar age to myself.
2	Speak to a shop assistant.
3	Ask a stranger the time.
4	Go up to an acquaintance and talk to them.
5	Go up to a group of friends and talk to them.
6	Go to a party or social occasion.
7	Go to a busy café and order a drink.
8	Ask a question during a talk or lecture.
9	Invite a friend for coffee.
10	Walk through a busy shopping centre.

Focus points

❋ Agoraphobia is often associated with panic attacks and can lead to avoidance of a range of normal activities until the sufferer's world becomes smaller and smaller.

❋ Agoraphobia is best treated with a plan that involves gradual exposure to the feared situation so that the sufferer 'habituates' or becomes used to the situation, and the anxiety associated with it dissipates.

❋ Social phobia is often linked to agoraphobia as both may involve avoidance of social situations.

❋ Cognitive restructuring is a vital component of any treatment plan for social phobia so that sufferers are able to 'catch' and replace any thinking errors which might result in misinterpretation of cues around them.

❋ Treating complex phobias takes time and effort, as lifelong habits need to be unlearned. Expect setbacks and be prepared for a long (and bumpy) journey!

7

Specific phobias

In this chapter you will learn:

▶ *What specific, or simple, phobias are*
▶ *About the ten most common specific phobias, including arachnophobia and fear of heights*
▶ *How to diagnose particular phobias*
▶ *How to deal with particular phobias*

How do you feel?

1 Do you have a phobia that is stopping you from leading
   a normal life?   Yes/No

2 Do you have to do things differently because of your phobia?   Yes/No

3 Have you read the earlier chapters (Chapters 1 and 4) on
   coping with phobias?   Yes/No

4 Are you ready to tackle your own phobia?   Yes/No

5 Will overcoming your phobia improve the quality of your life?   Yes/No

If you've answered mostly 'yes' then this chapter is for you.

This chapter will deal with the most common specific/simple phobias that people have presented with at my clinic over the years; these are, naturally, representative of the most common phobias within the general population, although the actual prevalence can vary. For example, one Dutch study in 2008 found heights to be the most common phobia, followed by animals (Depla, et al, 2008).

If you recall from Chapter 1 specific/simple phobias can be classified into four sub-types:

▶ Animal (fear of animals or creatures). These commonly include spiders, snakes, dogs, cats, bats, rats, cockroaches, mice, chickens, bees and insects.

▶ Environment (fear of environmental events). Common phobias in this category include thunder, lightning, heights, the dark etc.

▶ Medical – the most common medical phobias include fear of blood, injections, needles, vomiting, injury, doctors, hospitals etc.

▶ Situational phobias (fear of certain situations) include crowded places, public transport, flying, driving etc.

According to the 2008 Dutch study then, the most common phobias are as follows:

Phobia	Sub-type	Percentage with the phobia
Heights	Natural environment	19.1
Dogs or spiders	Animals	12.6
Enclosed spaces	Situational	9.5
Blood	Medical	9.5
Storms	Natural environment	7.0
Flying	Situational	6.9

We will now examine some of the more common phobias; for each phobia, there will be a brief explanation of the condition, a diagnostic quiz and suggestions for treatment.

Arachnophobia

The fear of spiders tends to affect women more than men. Some theorists believe that fear of spiders had important evolutionary benefits in that it was helpful for survival to fear venomous spiders. However, this theory is rather contentious since it is thought that there are very few species of spider which are actually dangerous to humans. In fact, countries that have the fewest dangerous spiders (like the UK) tend to have more sufferers of spider phobia when compared to countries with more poisonous spiders (like many countries in Africa).

Perhaps, then, in countries like the UK, spider phobias originated not with the danger of the spiders themselves, but with the diseases that they might carry. However, common flies probably carry (and have carried) just as many diseases but don't seem to have earned the same reputation as spiders in terms of phobias.

Spiders are one of the few modern phobias that have been with us since ancient times; our ancestors could not have feared lifts, escalators, needles or flying! Nor could they have very easily been afraid of heights (no tall buildings in those days!) or even public speaking. Snakes are probably the only other fear that has probably been around as long as spiders – but snake phobias are rarer because, in many parts of the world, the chances of encountering a snake are rather smaller than the chances of encountering a spider.

Remember this

It is very rare for spiders to be harmful to humans.

So, how to treat your spider phobia? Start by completing the following questionnaire aimed at diagnosing the severity and extent of your spider phobia:

Spider phobia questionnaire
How much do you agree with the following statements?

	1 Strongly agree	2 Somewhat agree	3 Somewhat disagree	4 Strongly disagree
I avoid going to parks or other places where there may be spiders.				
I avoid going into certain rooms in my house in case there are spiders.				
I find it hard to even say the word 'spider'.				
I would find it hard to look at a cartoon picture of a spider.				
I would find it hard to look at a picture of a real spider.				
I would find it hard to hold a toy spider in my hand.				
I would find it hard to watch someone else holding a real spider.				
I have to repeatedly check my bedroom for evidence of spiders before going to sleep.				
I would find it hard to watch a spider building a web.				
The thought of seeing a spider makes me anxious.				
The way spiders move is horrible.				
It is not natural to like spiders.				
Spiders are hideous creatures.				
I would not touch a dead spider even with a long stick.				

	1 Strongly agree	2 Somewhat agree	3 Somewhat disagree	4 Strongly disagree
I need other people to get rid of spiders for me.				
I avoid (or take great care with) certain fruits in case they attract spiders.				
Even if I knew a spider was not harmful, I would still be scared of it.				
I would rather be late for a meeting than take a route that might bring me into contact with spiders.				

The closer your score is to 18, the more spider phobic you are. You now need to devise a spider situational hierarchy (see Chapter 4 for more on creating situational hierarchies), which might look something like this:

Suggested situational hierarchy for spider phobia

Step	Task or situation	Score 0–100 BEFORE	Score 0–100 DURING	Score 0–100 AFTER
1	Look at cartoons of spiders.			
2	Look at pictures of real spiders.			
3	Hold toy spiders.			
4	Read stories about spiders.			
5	Write stories about spiders.			
6	Touch a dead spider with a long stick.			
7	Catch a spider in a glass.			
8	Go to places where there might be spiders.			
9	Stay in the same room as a spider.			

Of course, your own hierarchy might be different from this depending on exactly what you fear most.

Follow the advice in Chapter 4 (see Kai's case study in that chapter too) and in other chapters on dealing with the panic (e.g. Chapter 5) that can result from your close encounters with spiders. It might also be worth embarking on a spider handling session at your local zoo (see below).

'At Bristol Zoo Gardens we have responded to the demand for people wanting to get over their fear of spiders by offering a course, called "Living with spiders". Led by a counsellor and hypnotherapist and supported by a member of the Zoo Education team, the course takes place in the Zoo's Conservation Education Centre. You will join a small and personal group, with up to ten participants enjoying a relaxed, friendly atmosphere. The course lasts for up to four hours and includes a variety of approaches to help you, including talks, relaxation, hypnotherapy and an optional meeting with our friendly spiders.'

From the Bristol zoo website: http://www.bristolzoo.org.uk/phobia-courses-0

Acrophobia

Acrophobia (from the Greek, meaning 'summit') is an extreme or irrational fear of heights. This fear can lead to anxiety attacks and avoidance of high places, such as above the second or third floor in an office block.

Acrophobia can be dangerous, as sufferers can experience a panic attack in a high place and become too agitated to get themselves down safely. Some acrophobics also suffer from an urge to throw themselves off a high place, despite not being suicidal; they fear that they will actually throw themselves off a ledge or out of a window and will be unable to stop themselves from doing so.

Mythbuster
Height phobics fear that they will throw themselves off a tall building or jump out of the window. Treatment will help them learn that they won't carry out this irrational behaviour.

Height phobias tend to begin in late childhood or early adolescence. Unlike other phobias, height phobia rarely originates from some negative or traumatic incident; for example, no relationship has been found between children falling from a height and exhibiting height phobia (Boffino, et al, 2009). This suggests that, for some reason, people develop a fear of heights in the absence of any negative learning experience. As a result, some researchers suggest that there is an entirely different mechanism responsible for fear of heights than for other phobias, and that people with height phobias have difficulties with balance control which lead to acrophobic symptoms (Boffino, et al, 2009). In other words, it is hypothesized that people who have sensitivity to balance and thus feel uncomfortable in situations where they feel balance is important (e.g. in high places), might develop height phobia.

Height phobia questionnaire
How much do you agree with the following statements?

	1 Strongly agree	2 Somewhat agree	3 Somewhat disagree	4 Strongly disagree
I avoid going above the third floor of a building.				
I dislike going up escalators or staircases.				
I avoid going over bridges.				
I avoid motorway bridges.				
I fear that I will throw myself off a high place.				
I am afraid to sit close to a window in a high building.				
I am very aware of dizziness and/or my body swaying when I am at a high place.				

The nearer your score to 7, the more height phobic you are. Your situational hierarchy might look something like this:

Suggested situational hierarchy for height phobia

Step	Task or situation	Score 0–100 BEFORE	Score 0–100 DURING	Score 0–100 AFTER
1	Travel up an escalator			
2	Travel in a glass lift			
3	Walk along the middle of a low bridge			
4	Walk along a low bridge, but right at the edge			
5	Walk along a higher bridge to the middle and back again			
6	Walk from one end of a higher bridge to the other			
7	Walk to the edge of a higher bridge			
8	Walk to the window in a tall building			

Again, your own hierarchy might look different from this (follow the techniques outlined in Chapter 4 to develop your own hierarchy).

Cynophobia

The fear of dogs is often associated with specific personal experiences such as being bitten by a dog during childhood. Animal phobias tend to begin at an earlier age (early childhood) than other phobias. There are normally three ways in which a phobia can be acquired: direct conditioning, vicarious acquisition or instruction (see Chapter 1). For dogs then, this means that the phobic was probably either attacked by a dog or frightened by one (direct conditioning), observed another person being attacked or frightened (vicarious acquisition) or has been told that dogs are dangerous and are to be avoided (instruction).

Sometimes, dog phobics can't recall any particular reason to explain their fear and it could be that the original reason has been long forgotten. One study (reported in Hoffman and

Human, 2003) suggested that most animal phobics (68 per cent) couldn't actually recall an explanation for the onset of their phobia, while 23 per cent attributed it to direct conditioning. A further 4 per cent thought it was acquired by instruction, and 4 per cent thought it was vicarious learning.

Dog phobias are very common in children and can lead to a range of avoidance behaviours that can impact on normal day-to-day living (such as going to the park or taking a particular route to school).

Dog phobia questionnaire
Use the following questionnaire to establish whether you have a dog phobia (or to what extent you might have one). If it is your child who has the phobia, complete it on their behalf.

	1 Strongly agree	2 Somewhat agree	3 Somewhat disagree	4 Strongly disagree
I avoid going to the park in case dogs are there.				
I prefer to change my route in order to avoid dogs.				
Watching dogs on television or in films bothers me.				
I cross the road to avoid dogs.				
Reading stories about dogs bothers me.				
The thought of touching a dog fills me with fear.				
I believe dogs are dangerous.				
Hearing dogs bark fills me with fear.				
Large dogs are particularly frightening.				
I tend to notice dogs' eyes or how they walk.				

The nearer your score to 10, the more phobic you probably are.

In addition to the usual situational hierarchy for treating dog phobia, it is useful to undergo some education about dog behaviour. This is particularly useful for phobics who believe that the cause of their phobia is their perception of the danger of dogs. Education can help teach dog phobics about those situations where a dog might present a danger (e.g. looking for signs of aggression) and those where they might not. It can also be useful to seek out 'helping dogs' such as guide dogs as these can be helpful, especially with children, in overcoming fears.

Suggested situational hierarchy for dog phobia

Step	Task or situation	Score 0–100 BEFORE	Score 0–100 DURING	Score 0–100 AFTER
1	Look at pictures of dogs			
2	Watch films featuring dogs			
3	Read stories about dogs			
4	Be in the same room as a small dog			
5	Stroke a small dog (under the supervision of trusted owner)			
6	Stroke a larger dog (under the supervision of trusted owner)			
7	Walk past dogs that are on a lead in the street			
8	Go to the park where dogs might be off the lead			

Again, your own hierarchy might look different from this, but this one should give you an idea of how to go about creating one (see also Chapter 4).

Astraphobia

This is the fear of thunder and lightning, also known as brontophobia, tonitrophobia or ceraunophobia. This is a 'natural environment' sub-type and is especially common in young children. Symptoms (similar for all other extreme phobias) include panic attack, difficulty in breathing, rapid heartbeat, sweaty palms, and nausea. Sometimes these feelings can be overwhelming.

Many people try to cope with their fear by hiding from the storm in places where they can't see or hear it. Sufferers may obsess with weather forecasts and even avoid going outside if there is any threat of a storm. Sufferers can even become agoraphobic if they start avoiding going out.

Use the following questionnaire to examine the extent of your thunder/lightning phobia.

Thunder/lightning phobia questionnaire
How much do you agree with the following statements?

	1 Strongly agree	2 Somewhat agree	3 Somewhat disagree	4 Strongly disagree
I check the weather forecast for storms before going out.				
I will not go out if there is the possibility of a thunderstorm.				
On hearing thunder or seeing lightning, I run and hide somewhere.				
My phobia prevents me living a normal life.				
Thunderstorms make me very anxious and panicky.				
The loudness of the thunder is particularly scary.				
I fear being struck by lightning.				
I think the chances of being struck by lightning are quite high.				

The closer your score to 8, the more likely you are to be phobic about thunderstorms.

This phobia is actually quite difficult to treat because it is hard to build up gradual exposure to something so unpredictable. It should be noted that many children fear thunderstorms without this being classed as an actual phobia (see Chapter 1 for advice on whether a fear is a phobia or just a fear). The first point of treatment for a thunderstorm phobia is education: learning about how thunder and lightning happen, for example, can take some of the fear away. Many phobics are less frightened of the lightning (which is potentially dangerous) than the thunder, which is so loud that it can be very scary, even though it is not dangerous. Lack of understanding of the phenomenon, especially with children, can help feed the fear.

Key idea

Thunder phobias can often be helped by learning about the science of how thunder and lightning occur.

Another technique is to obtain a CD of thunderstorms and listen to it over and over again until it no longer evokes fear. Watching thunderstorms on TV or in films can help too. Apart from these techniques, you would need to look out for a thunderstorm then set up a situational hierarchy as follows:

Suggested situational hierarchy for thunderstorm phobia

Step	Task or situation	Score 0–100 BEFORE	Score 0–100 DURING	Score 0–100 AFTER
1	Learn about how thunderstorms happen, what causes thunder and lightning etc.			
2	Listen to a recording of thunder			
3	Watch films of thunderstorms			
4	Listen to a real thunderstorm from the safety of the house			
5	Watch a real thunderstorm from the safety of the window			

Trypanophobia

This is the fear of injections; like many phobias, this fear often goes untreated because people avoid the triggering object and situation. This is part of the medical sub-type; it is very common and often extends to fear of any medical procedure. Approximately 80 per cent of people with a fear of needles report that a close relative exhibits the same disorder. The phobia actually makes evolutionary sense; before the days of inoculations etc., it would have been sensible to avoid anything that might pierce the skin.

There are distinct types of needle phobia:

▶ Vasovagal

The most common type of needle phobia, affecting 50 per cent of sufferers, is an inherited reflex reaction. People who suffer from vasovagal needle phobia fear the sight, thought or feeling of needles or needle-like objects. The primary symptom of vasovagal fear is fainting due to a decrease in blood pressure. Initially, there is an acceleration of heart rate and raised blood pressure when encountering the needle. This is followed by a rapid plunge in both heart rate and blood pressure, sometimes leading to fainting. These symptoms make up what is known as the *vasovagal syncope reaction*. Many people who suffer from fainting during needle procedures report no conscious fear of the needle procedure itself, but a great fear of the vasovagal syncope reaction. A study in the medical journal *Circulation* concluded that in many patients with this condition (as well as patients with the broader range of blood/injury phobias), an initial episode of vasovagal syncope during a needle procedure may be the primary cause of needle phobia rather than any basic fear of needles (Accurso, et al, 2001).

▶ Associative

Associative needle phobia is the next most common type, affecting about 30 per cent of needle phobics. This type is the classic specific phobia in which a traumatic event, such as an extremely painful medical procedure or witnessing a family member or friend undergo one, causes the patient to associate all procedures involving needles with the original negative experience.

▶ Resistive

This form of needle phobia affects around 20 per cent of sufferers. Resistive needle phobia occurs when the underlying fear involves not simply needles or injections but also being controlled or restrained. It typically stems from a repressive upbringing or poor handling of prior needle procedures, i.e. with forced physical or emotional restraint.

▶ Hyperalgesic

This form of needle phobia affects around 10 per cent of sufferers. Hyperalgesic fear of needles is another form that does not have as much to do with fear of the actual needle. Patients with this form have an inherited hypersensitivity to pain, or hyperalgesia. To them, the pain of an injection is unbearably great and many cannot understand how anyone can tolerate such procedures.

Needle/injection phobia questionnaire
This questionnaire can help you to identify the type of needle phobia that you have (V = vasovagal, A = associative, R = resistive and H = hyperalgesic)

Tick all those that apply:	
I have had a previous injection and fainted.	V
It isn't the needle I fear so much, but the fainting.	V
I had a very traumatic experience with an injection that started my fear.	A
I witnessed someone else having a very bad experience with an injection.	A
The whole idea of being restrained in some way in order to have the injection fills me with fear.	R
Not being able to move or escape during an injection is what scares me the most.	R
The pain associated with the needle is what gives me the most fear.	H
I can't understand how anyone can tolerate the pain of injections.	H

Needle phobias are a little tricky to treat without access to both needles and medical practitioners able to carry out inert (i.e. containing saline solution, for example, rather than real inoculations) injection procedures. In the following hierarchy, the earlier steps can be carried out without expert intervention.

Suggested situational hierarchy for needle phobia

Step	Task or situation	Score 0–100 BEFORE	Score 0–100 DURING	Score 0–100 AFTER
1	Talk about injections and needles.			
2	Look at needles.			
3	Hold a needle			
4	Watch someone else having an injection.			
5 *	Have a brief procedure involving quick piercing of the skin.			
6 *	Have an inert injection.			

*Seeing a professional can be useful for needle phobics who want to go to the next level and actually get injected (either with saline or with the real thing, e.g. a vaccine).

Key idea

Needle phobics can benefit from watching other people have injections (where possible).

Pteromerhanophobia/aviophobia

This is the fear of flying. Commercial flight has become an important, even essential, part of modern life, yet flying continues to cause a significant proportion of the public to feel anxious. Fear of flying seems to contradict the facts: for example, driving in a car is statistically many times more dangerous (although there is also the perception that, while car crashes are far more likely to happen, we have more chance of surviving them). A report in *The Independent* in August 2009 claimed that 'statistically speaking, every row of three seats on a commercial aeroplane contains at least one passenger who'd really rather not be there' (interestingly, the article online was surrounded by airline ads).

The fear of flying may be created by various factors:

▶ a fear of closed-in spaces (claustrophobia), such as that of an aircraft cabin;

▶ a fear of heights (acrophobia);

- a feeling of not being in control (since a passenger is not piloting the plane and can't get out at will);

- previous traumatizing experiences while on a flight;

- fear of hijacking or terrorism;

- fear of deep vein thrombosis;

- fear of turbulence;

- fear of having a medical emergency while in the air;

- fear of having a panic attack.

Some experts blame the media as a major factor behind fear of flying, claiming that the media sensationalize airline crashes (and the high casualty rate per incident), in comparison to the perceived scant attention given the massive number of isolated car crashes. For example, only multiple car pile-ups tend to reach the media's attention, whereas every plane crash is front page news for many weeks (because of the large number of fatalities). This creates the impression that plane crashes are more likely to occur than they really are (the so-called 'availability bias', which means that events that are more available to us in our memories tend to be perceived as happening more frequently).

Mythbuster

Travelling by air is not more dangerous than travelling by car – it is just that air disasters get a lot more media coverage so are subject to 'availability bias'.

For many people, it is the feeling of a lack of control felt that gives rise to the fear; most of us have no idea how a plane works and just how it stays in the air, and this lack of control can be hard to accept. We might not know how cars work either, but we do know how to drive them.

Fear of flying is just as irrational as any other fear because our chances of actually being in a plane crash are so low (according to the book *Overcoming Your Fear of Flying* by Robert Bor, we have more chance of being kicked to death by a donkey). But, of course, this rational explanation will not help real flying phobics whose fear is emotional rather than rational.

Normally, when treating a phobia, we build a situational hierarchy and work our way up the successive rungs of the ladder as explained in Chapter 4. With flying phobia, this is hard to do without easy access to a Boeing 747. Many airlines do run 'fear of flying' courses which offer education and exposure to a plane (real or simulated) but these courses are often very expensive. A self-help programme including the following elements can work for many people:

▶ Learn about the mechanics of flying – how the plane flies, stays in the air and what those scary noises mean (see below).

Mythbuster

Aeroplanes can fly safely to their destination even if one engine fails. An aeroplane can glide for 30 minutes before landing, even without any engines working. Planes can even land in zero visibility.

Planes are also fitted with collision avoidance systems as a back-up to air traffic control.

They have weather radars so as to avoid bad conditions, but are still equipped to fly through storms. Lightning can strike an aircraft, but because it's not connected to the ground it leaves the plane unscathed.

And aeroplanes have enough fuel on board to fly to several other landing alternatives.

(Taken from *Daily Mail* 14 June 2010: 'How to...cure a fear of flying' by Tom Mitchelson)

▶ Focus on the end goal. Being unable to fly is restrictive so if you really want to visit a far-off place, or family, focus on that end goal.

▶ Learn the deep muscle relaxation technique expounded in Chapter 3. You will need these when you start exposing yourself to flying.

▶ Start going to the airport for visits. You might feel very anxious even doing that at first. Watch some of the thousands of people who fly every day. Watch the planes take off and land. Do this until you feel relaxed and comfortable.

▶ Now book a short flight of, say, 30 minutes. Practise the relaxation technique before and during the flight. Take distractors with you: water, chewing gum and easy reading, for example, and remind yourself of the end-goal. Talk to the cabin crew – explain that you are fearful and have booked this flight to try to overcome your fears. They will probably go out of their way to reassure you during the flight. Don't drink alcohol!

Key idea

Flying phobias can be helped by understanding the mechanics of how aircraft fly, the sounds they make and the science of how they stay airborne.

See also the material on flying in Chapter 4.

Mysophobia

This is the fear of germs or dirt. It is often related to obsessive–compulsive disorder which is discussed in greater detail in Chapter 9. It is normal and prudent to be concerned about issues such as cross-contamination of foods, exposure to the bodily fluids of others and maintaining good hygiene. However, if you suffer from mysophobia, these normal concerns can become so severe that they take over your life, and you find it difficult to function or lead a normal life. Read Chapter 9 if this sounds like you.

Emetophobia

Emetophobia is an excessive or irrational fear of vomiting or of being around others who are vomiting. It is one of the most common specific phobias, with more women than men suffering from it. In survey research, six percent of the US population claim to fear being sick, although a much smaller number suffer from actual emetophobia, which manifests itself through a variety of phobic behaviours.

It is unknown what exactly causes emetophobia to develop, but the accepted theory says that it can result from a traumatic incident of vomiting between the ages of six and ten. Most emetophobics claim they can stop themselves vomiting, and a survey of an internet group of emetophobics found that the average member had last vomited at least 12 years earlier. On average, it is suggested that most emetophobics have been sick five times or fewer in their lives.

Emetophobics are known to go to great lengths to avoid people who may be sick or where a threat of infection is perceived. Some emetophobics will avoid being in public places where they fear people may vomit or where they think there may be a higher probability of someone vomiting (such as a bar or a nightclub or hospital). Almost half of all female emetophobics avoid becoming pregnant (Davidson, Boyle and Lauchlan, 2008). They will experience panic attacks when faced with the possibility of encountering someone vomiting and may be extremely selective in their attention to cues about vomiting (for example, being highly alert to signs that someone might be about to vomit). They find it hard to even talk about vomiting.

Case study

Lucy was a young girl of eight who presented at my clinic because of her fear of vomiting. It started at school in assembly when another child vomited right in front of her, which Lucy found horrific. It made her feel so traumatized that she felt ill and sick herself and was in tears. She was sent home by the school and she stayed away for two weeks – each time she came back, she would be in tears and start shaking and claiming she was ill. Her mother was summoned to collect her each time. Once she was home, she was fine. Eventually, they came to me to try to sort her out. We started by talking about how watching the child throw up in front of her made her feel. We talked over and over again about it so that, eventually, she didn't feel so anxious just talking about it, or thinking about it.

We then moved on to looking at pictures of people who look like they might be sick. She found this very hard but eventually realized that looking at these pictures wouldn't actually make her sick – even if she felt nauseous. She realized that she could cope with the unpleasant feelings she felt – even though she didn't like them, she learned that nothing terrible would happen and that she wouldn't throw up as she feared she might. This was enough to get her back to school – she was still nervous if anyone looked ill and got a bit panicky, but was able to cope. Eventually, her phobia subsided and she was able to enjoy normal life again.

Nearly all emetophobics will practise eating habits that may seem strange if noticed by non-emetophobics, ranging from pickiness to superstitions about foods to anorexia. Such eating habits may include refusing to eat any food that they have touched with their hands (as opposed to cutlery) and eating their food in a specific order. Others may eat in a way they believe will minimize the chance of vomiting or nausea. Emetophobics often follow strict diet regimes that consists of 'safe foods' and foods that are least likely to cause food poisoning – meat and dairy products for example will often be avoided or abstained from completely. Emetophobics will often avoid foods that they ate on or around the time they last vomited, for fear that eating them again will either bring back disturbing memories, or through a superstitious belief that eating the same food may lead them to vomit again. Additionally, many emetophobics experience gastrointestinal problems such as IBS or lactose intolerance, and pay careful attention to their digestive systems, believing that any discomfort or pressure will lead to gastroenteritis.

Most emetophobics fear vomiting themselves, but in some cases, it has been claimed that the fear of seeing other people vomit can induce an even greater phobic response than if they were to be sick themselves. They may cope by:

▶ avoiding sick people;

▶ avoiding children (including their own if they are poorly);

▶ avoiding hospitals;

▶ avoiding other places where people might be sick such as buses, planes etc.;

▶ having unusual eating habits;

▶ being obsessive about hygiene;

▶ obsessively checking the use-by dates on food stuffs.

Vomiting phobia questionnaire

How much do you agree with the following statements?

	1 Strongly agree	2 Somewhat agree	3 Somewhat disagree	4 Strongly disagree
I worry a lot about vomiting.				
I worry a lot about other people vomiting near me.				
I avoid people sometimes because of my fear of vomiting.				
I try to stop myself from vomiting if I am ill.				
I try not to even think about vomiting.				
I can't say the word 'vomit' without feeling uncomfortable.				
If I read or see something about vomiting I turn the page quickly.				
I avoid alcohol in case it makes me vomit.				
I avoid eating certain food groups because of my fear.				
I am obsessive about checking use-by dates on food.				
I get panic attacks when I see someone vomiting.				
Seeing someone vomit would make me throw up too.				
I avoid fast rides at theme parks because of my fear.				
I don't eat in restaurants much because of my fear.				

The closer your score is to 14, the stronger your phobia would appear to be. Treating emetophobics is difficult using the traditional 'hierarchy' approach (systematic desensitization) because it is unethical to try to induce vomiting (as this may be harmful) or to expose them to other people vomiting (this might be unethical towards the other person concerned). However, recent research has suggested that emetophobia is associated with issues to do with control. It has been found that emetophobics have a higher internal locus of control than non-emetophobics, which means that they consider most aspects of their lives to be within their own control (Davidson, Boyle and Lauchlan, 2008). They believe that they can and must control not only their own ability to vomit, but also many other aspects of their lives. The fear of vomiting then, may be more to do with worry about their own lack of control (inability to resist the violent urge to vomit) than actual fear of any other element of the process. Treating emetophobia then, might include examining the need for control and helping the phobic person relax their need for constant control.

Having said that, severe emetophobics can benefit from a situational hierarchy that stops short of actual exposure to vomit. It might look something like this:

Step	Task or situation	Score 0–100 BEFORE	Score 0–100 DURING	Score 0–100 AFTER
1	Looking at the word 'vomit'			
2	Saying the word 'vomit'			
3	Reading and saying other related words such as spew, throw up, retch etc.			
4	Reading about vomiting			
5	Looking at pictures of people looking unwell			
6	Looking at pictures of people before and after they vomit			
7.	Looking at pictures of people being sick			
8.	Listening to sounds of people being sick			

You should obtain these sounds and images by asking a trusted friend to search the internet (including YouTube) for appropriate images. Because this is difficult – your friend has to take care not to present you with an image that is too anxiety-producing for you – this phobia is harder to treat with self-help. An experienced therapist will have access to appropriate resources to help you.

Dental phobia

Dental phobia is very common and there are a number of sub-phobias that might account for it including: fear of needles, fear of choking (more on this in Chapter 8), fear of embarrassment, fear of pain, fear of the drill and fear of not having control. A survey by the British Dental Association showed that 25 per cent of people suffer from anxiety before visiting the dentist. This means, then, that 25 per cent of the population must either try their best to cope with their dental phobia, or risk their oral health by not visiting the dentist at all. Dental phobias are often exacerbated by the following:

▶ discomfort of having to open mouth wide;

▶ tilting chair back;

▶ being unable to talk and explain how you are feeling;

▶ noise of the drill;

▶ not knowing what is happening;

▶ unexpected things happening to you;

▶ pain.

Some of these problems can be helped by having a sympathetic dentist who keeps you informed about what is happening, doesn't do anything unexpected, allows you more control, explains procedures carefully and allows you to proceed at your own pace where possible. Relaxation techniques can help too, as can distraction (e.g. listening to music). But really, to treat a dental phobia, you need access to a sympathetic dentist who is experienced with phobic patients.

Key idea

There are many dentists these days who specialize in dental phobias and they can be very effective in helping even the most committed dental phobic overcome their fear.

A useful website is http://www.dentalphobia.co.uk/

Lift/elevator phobia

This is a common fear and is associated with claustrophobia (fear of enclosed spaces). The sufferer usually fears being unable to get out or escape, rather than a fear of the lift crashing. Most lift phobics that I deal with are more worried about being trapped in the lift than about the lift itself being dangerous – although they fear that something catastrophic will happen to them while trapped, like a heart attack, for which they will be unable to get help.

A good start to dealing with a lift phobia is education. Finding out how lifts work and what safety/emergency mechanisms are in place can be beneficial. It is also useful to find out how long you are likely to be stuck in a lift if the worst did happen (see the advice in Chapter 4 and the case study below).

Case study

Paul came to my clinic about his lift phobia. He had had this phobia for as long as he could remember and his dad had it too, as well as other family members. He had managed until now, at the age of 36, to cope with the phobia, by managing to avoid lifts without too much difficulty. The problem now was that he was due to start a new job that was on the tenth floor of an office building. Not only that, the job was such that he had to go out and about visiting other clients who might also be high up in office blocks. There was no way he was going to be able to use the stairs and avoid lifts. He realized that if he didn't get his lift phobia sorted out, he would lose the job. So, he was really determined to get cured!

I started by teaching him relaxation techniques and we also examined his cognitions (what he thought would happen to him). I taught him that his panic would eventually go and nothing would happen to him, even if a lift did break down. We devised a 'distraction' kit to carry around with him in case the lift ever got stuck (because, of course, there is no guarantee that it won't); this included something to read (a newspaper) and a bottle of water.

We started out with glass lifts and although he was terrified and panicky, he managed to go in – first with me and eventually by himself. We spent an hour just going up and down in a glass lift until he was used to it and no longer anxious. Once he learned that the panic would go, we could move onto other lifts and within three sessions he was able to get into any lift on his own. At first I would be on the other end of the phone for him, but eventually he didn't need that anymore. We arranged a final session in a large 30-floor hotel but he rang to cancel – he managed to do it on his own and didn't need me anymore! Success!

More on treating lift phobics, including a suggested situational hierarchy, is given in Chapter 4.

Focus points

* All phobias can be classified as either animal-based, medical-based, situational or environmental.
* The starting point for treating most phobias is some sort of diagnostic awareness of the type and severity of phobia you have.
* Learning the facts or science behind the thing you fear can help to combat it, since we often fear what we don't understand.
* Gradual exposure to the object of your fear is always the way forward.
* You must ensure that you are totally relaxed and unanxious before you attempt to move up the next rung of your hierarchical ladder.

Anxiety conditions in children

In this chapter you will learn:

▶ *About common fears and phobias in children*

▶ *How to determine whether a child will 'grow out of' their phobia or whether it is a more serious problem*

▶ *What causes childhood phobias*

▶ *Tips to prevent anxieties from becoming a major problem*

▶ *How to treat childhood phobias*

How do you feel?

1 Do you worry whether your child's anxieties and worries are normal?
Yes/No

2 Do you want to be able to nip anxieties in the bud before they become more serious? Yes/No

3 Do your child's anxieties stop you or them from leading a normal life? Yes/No

4 Does your child have problems going to school because of their anxieties? Yes/No

5 Does your child spend an excessive amount of time engaged in rituals or repetitive behaviours? Yes/No

The more 'yes' answers, the more likely it is that you will find this chapter useful.

Childhood anxiety and phobias are very common. Children experience a range of fears and anxieties over the course of their development and much of this is quite normal. For example, it is common for small children to be afraid of the dark, of being alone, of unpredictable animals (like dogs or spiders) or of unpredictable and confusing events (like thunder). All these things threaten their feelings of security and safety, so it is natural that they make kids anxious.

For most children, these fears are short-lived and are not sufficiently severe for them to be a major problem. For example, a child of five might not stay downstairs in a house alone while the rest of the family are upstairs, but by the age of seven or eight, they probably will. Their refusal to stay downstairs alone at five does not really limit their life much, nor impinge too much on the rest of the family. If they are still like this at ten, to the extent that they won't even sleep in their own room at night or let you leave them alone in a room, then this might signify a phobia.

Remember this

It is very common for children to have fears and anxieties, and most children will grow out of them.

How do you know if your child's fear and anxieties are normal for their age?

Newborns typically fear falling and loud noises; their 'shock' response is normal and typical at that age. Fear of strangers begins as early as six months and persists until the age of two or three – or older. Pre-school children usually fear being separated from their parents; they may also be afraid of large animals, dark places, masks and 'monsters'. At this age it is common for them to be afraid of sleeping alone, or with the light off, or without checking under the bed for monsters. Older children may worry about death in the family, failure at school, and events in the news such as wars, terrorist attacks and kidnappings. Adolescents have sexual and social anxieties, and concerns about their own and the world's future. Such anxieties only become a problem if they persist and cause serious distress, affect the family relationships or dynamics, or interfere with a child's development or education.

▶ **Common fears of an infant or toddler**

These tend to be reflexive:

▶ loud noises or sudden movements;

▶ large, looming objects;

▶ strangers;

▶ separation;

▶ fear of toilets (may occur during toilet training).

Case study

At four years old Jacob was toilet trained and doing well, but he didn't like loud noises. This is common for children of that age, but Jacob became frightened of noisy hand-dryers in public toilets. The summer before he was due to start school this became more of a problem as he began to refuse to go into any public toilets that had hand-dryers – however quiet or noisy they were. It got to the stage where he wouldn't visit the toilet at all when he was out, preferring to either wet himself or use a bush! When he started school after the summer, he discovered that the school toilets had hand-dryers too – and he wouldn't use them. Obviously at this stage, the problem had escalated into something that needed immediate treatment.

Jacob and his mum visited my clinic. Because Jacob was so young, I couldn't do much in the way of education or explaining about phobias, but his age did mean that he would respond well to rewards. We talked together about how it wasn't nice if he wet himself (which he agreed with) so that I could ensure he was motivated to change. I gave him a lovely notebook and a set of puffy stickers, and told him that he would have some very easy things to do and each time he did them, he would get a lovely sticker in his book. When he had ten stickers, his mum would buy him a small present (such as a chocolate bar). He was excited by this but wary about the tasks. I explained that the first task was to go and find toilets with noisy hand-dryers, open the door and stand at the entrance. Every time he did this, he would get a sticker.

He went off with his mum and they did this for a few days. Once it became easy for him, they progressed so that he had to stand in the room to get his sticker – this was harder, especially if the hand-dryer was on, but a few days later he had accomplished this. He then had to move closer to the hand-dryer for his sticker. He was actually enjoying the game and, within two weeks, was able to use hand-dryers himself! In fact, he loved them! He would go on days out with mum around the shopping centre, searching for the noisiest hand-dryer!

▶ Common fears during pre-school years

This tends to be the most fearful group as their imagination starts to develop but they lack the cognitive awareness to rationalize their fears. Remember that they can't distinguish between imaginary creatures and real ones, so their fear of monsters, for example, is very real to them. Common fears in this age group include:

▶ the dark;

▶ noises at night;

▶ masks;

▶ monsters and ghosts (imaginary creatures);

▶ animals, such as dogs.

▶ Common fears during school years

By the age of five, a child's main fear might be of getting lost or being separated from a parent; this can make them very clingy. They still have a vivid imagination so might be less scared of 'monsters' in general, but more scared of going into the basement in case some ghost is hiding there. Fears tend to lessen by the age of seven, though social fears and performance anxiety (e.g. about school and exams) tend to kick in then.

Common fears in this age group include:

▶ snakes and spiders;

▶ storms and natural disasters;

▶ being at home alone (older children);

▶ fear of a teacher who's angry;

▶ scary news or TV shows;

▶ injury, illness, doctors, or death;

▶ fear of failure and rejection.

Thus, fears that are not age-appropriate, are long-lasting and that severely impact on the child (or their family's) normal existence, might be cause for concern. A ten-year-old who runs away from the Hoover or who refuses to go to the toilet is concerning, but a two-year-old with these symptoms is not.

Quiz: decide if your child's fear is a normal stage of development, or potentially a phobia that requires further input.

Does your child's fear seem age-appropriate?	Yes = 0	No = 1
Do other children their age have similar fears?	Yes = 0	No = 1
Does the school or nursery think your child's fears are unusual?	Yes = 1	No = 0
Does your child's response to the source of their fear seem excessive?	Yes = 1	No = 0
Does their fear mean that you have to run your family life differently?	Yes = 1	No = 0
Does their fear stop them doing things other children their age do?	Yes = 1	No = 0
Does their fear impact on your family life?	Yes = 1	No = 0

The more your total score nears 7, the more likely it is that your child has a phobia rather than a normal childhood fear.

Remember this

Fears that are not age-appropriate and that severely impact on your child's or your family's life, might indicate a cause for concern.

Common childhood phobias/anxieties

Specific phobias are quite common in children, occurring in around 5 per cent of kids (King and Ollendick, 1997), and are more prevalent in girls than in boys (as discussed in Chapter 7). There are thought to be three 'pathways' accounting for why children develop phobias:

▶ Direct conditioning/traumatic experience (e.g. a child being attacked by a dog)

▶ Modelling (e.g. the child observes their mother being fearful of lifts)

▶ Instruction (e.g. the child hears older siblings talk about how much they hate school).

Interestingly, direct conditioning is thought to be the least common way that phobias are learned (except for choking phobias; see later in this chapter). Modelling is thought by some researchers to be the most significant factor in the development of childhood phobias.

▶ Top tips to prevent anxieties becoming more serious

Normal childhood anxieties can develop into full-blown phobias but generally they don't. Often, there is little that you as a parent can do to stop phobias developing, but sometimes the way you react to your child's anxieties can make a difference. Here are some tips:

▶ Don't ridicule their fears. Being afraid of monsters in the wardrobe may seem ridiculous to you, but it is not to the child. Laughing at them or making fun of them will only cause them to associate more negative feelings with the source of their fear.

- Humour them. Check the wardrobe for monsters but do it in a way that shows you are proving to your child there is no monster – not to yourself.

- Don't frighten them further by suggesting, even in jest, that they are right to be afraid. Suggestions that 'god is angry' as an explanation for thunder, for example, is not likely to help them.

- Reassure them when there is nothing to fear. Remind them of why they need not be afraid e.g. 'That dog is on a lead so can't reach you', 'I am not going anywhere', or 'Look, the light makes shadows and they look like people but they're not'.

- Find stories about the things they fear – this can show good modelling behaviour (e.g. how another child overcame their fear) but also 'desensitize' them to talking about the source of their fear.

- Model brave behaviour. Show them that you are not afraid because there is nothing to be afraid of. If they see you trembling with fear in a lift, they will learn that lifts are something to be afraid of.

Remember this

Ridiculing or laughing at a child's fears is likely to make them more anxious, not less.

▶ How to explain panic attacks to children

If your child has a phobia or severe anxiety disorder they are likely to suffer from panic attacks. It is important to explain what is happening to them, as panic attacks can be terrifying for an adult, never mind a child. The following information can be given or read out to your younger child (adolescents can probably utilize the material in this book).

'Lots of people have panic attacks – grown-ups as well as children. Panic attacks can make you feel hot and sweaty, you might feel like you are choking or can't breathe, or dizzy like you might fall over. You might feel that something terrible will happen to you. Panic attacks feel horrible and people who have them will often try to do anything to stop them having another one. This means that they often avoid, or won't go near, things that might give them these horrible feelings. Some children and grown-ups won't go near dogs or spiders and they might not even go to places where they might see a dog or spider, just in case. Some children get these scary feelings when they go to school, so they don't even want to go to school. If you get these feelings so much that they are stopping you do things that children your age should do, then we need to do something to make you feel better.

One way to help is to not run away from things that give you these panic attacks. This can be very hard because all you want to do is get away! But, if you manage to stay, you will find that the horrible feelings will go on their own and that nothing terrible will happen to you. You have to learn this yourself though and the best way is to start in a small way. For example, if you are scared of spiders, start by looking at pictures of spiders. Don't try to hold a spider straight away!'

The rest of this chapter will examine four of the most common childhood anxiety disorders.

SCHOOL PHOBIA

School phobia, the term used to describe the fear that some children have in attending school, affects about five per cent of the school-age population (Chitiyo and Wheeler, 2006). School fear has been defined as an 'irrational fear or anxiety about attending school' (Chitiyo and Wheeler, 2006). Something about the school environment elicits an extreme fear reaction in the child. This is an important point, since it is rarely the 'school' itself that causes the fear, but rather some aspect to do with the school experience. This could be centred around the other children, the pressure to perform in some way, the teachers, the gym, getting changed for PE, or the playground etc.

Some researchers believe that school phobia is more to do with the fear of being away from the security offered by the parent or home, than to do with fear of school itself. Here, school phobia is viewed as an extension of separation anxiety which is exhibited when the child fears being apart from their care-giver (which is a normal fear for very small children).

School phobia should be distinguished from school refusal or truancy. The phobic child usually differs from the truant in that:

▶ They are often a good student, or were, until their phobia began.

▶ They often prefer to stay at home rather than go to other places.

▶ They may remain away from school for long periods rather than only intermittently.

▶ The parents are very aware of, and involved in, their absence.

Mythbuster

Children with school phobia are not truanting and are often good students.

School phobia doesn't seem to be more prevalent in any one gender, or at any particular age (although there is often a peak at school entry age of five to seven years) or social group. Most research suggests that school phobics tend to be of average or above average intelligence (Chitiyo and Wheeler, 2006).

School phobia can have a devastating impact if left untreated. Most researchers suggest that children with school phobia exhibit the following four personality characteristics (Chitiyo and Wheeler, 2006) which, left untreated, can lead to long-term problems later on:

▶ acute anxiety;

▶ determined attempts to manipulate the parent into allowing them to stay at home;

▶ depression and unhappiness;

▶ an unrealistic self-image (because of the continuous attention being given to them).

Of course, there is also the impact on the child's education of missing so much class time.

▶ School phobia questionnaire

Most children with 'school phobia' have a particular area of concern that causes their fear, so it is important to understand what the specific issue is for your child. Use this questionnaire in order to unpick exactly what is at the root of your child's school phobia.

Which of the following are areas of concern to your child?

Being away from Mummy/Daddy	
Getting lost	
Something happening to Mummy/Daddy while separated from them	
Not being collected at the end of the day	
Being hurt at school	
Not having needs met at school	
Being hungry/thirsty at school	
Being sick/ill at school	
Not knowing what to do at school	
Being shouted at while at school	
Doing something wrong at school	
The other children	
Being alone at school	
Having to do a test	
Having to read aloud	
The school being noisy	
The smell of the school	
The feeling of being trapped at school	
The school bell	
Aspects to do with PE (e.g. getting changed)	
A particular piece of equipment at school	
A teacher	
Worry about having a panic attack (usually in older children)	

Once you know the areas of greatest concern you can look at how to tackle your school phobic child.

▶ Treating school phobia

Forcing the child to go to school or using punishments is usually counter-productive. Cognitive behavioural therapy is often the most successful route, and the usual gradual exposure approach is best used. This requires collaboration with the school and allowances to be made to accommodate the child during their graduated exposure to school life. For example, a child's situational hierarchy might look like this:

Step	Task or situation
1	Stand outside the school grounds.
2	Step inside the school grounds.
3	Gradually get nearer to the school entrance.
4	Step into the school building with a parent when the school is not in session.
5	Go nearer and nearer to a classroom with a parent (when the school is not in session).
6	Repeat Steps 4 and 5 when the school is in session.
7	Sit in a classroom near the door with a parent outside the door (in view) for an 'enjoyable' and distracting session such as art.
8	The parent moves further away and the child remains for five minutes.
9	Increase the time the child spends in the classroom.

See Chapter 4 for more on graded exposure and situational hierarchies.

Key idea

Graduated entry to school, with the school's cooperation, is much more effective at treating school phobia than trying to force the child to go to school.

Reward systems can be utilized with young children to encourage adherence to the programme; for example, stickers can be used which accumulate to be swapped for prizes. However, as mentioned earlier, punishments should never be used for non-compliance – the programme should go at the child's pace and progress at comfortable rates for them. Many children want to return to the classroom but some see no reason to and are happier at home. These children may need greater incentives to comply with the programme.

SOCIAL PHOBIA

It is estimated that around four per cent of children (from age 11) exhibit social phobia, which is similar to adult social phobia (see Chapter 6). Symptoms, however, may be slightly different for children, and might include acute fear of being asked a question in class, being asked to read out loud in class, or taking part in extra-curricular activities. Social phobia is usually diagnosed after the age of 11; before this, there may appear to be overlaps with school phobia, or the child may be labelled as shy.

There are two main types of social phobia in children: performance-based and interaction-based.

Examples of performance-based social phobia	Examples of interaction-based social phobia
Reading out loud in class	Talking to classmates
Being asked a question in class	Talking to teachers
Walking into a room full of people	Going to social events
Carrying a dinner tray across the canteen (fear of falling)	Dating
Eating in front of others	Working in a group
Performing, e.g. music or in a school play	Expressing opinion

Children can have one or both of these types.

Remember this

Social phobia can involve fear of performing or fear based on social interactions, or even both.

Child social phobia questionnaire
How much does your child agree with the following statements?

	1 Strongly agree	2 Somewhat agree	3 Somewhat disagree	4 Strongly disagree
I don't know what to say when teachers talk to me.				
I don't know what to say or how to behave when other children talk to me.				
I am scared to say or do the wrong thing.				
I am worried that people will laugh at me.				

	1 Strongly agree	2 Somewhat agree	3 Somewhat disagree	4 Strongly disagree
I think people talk about me behind my back.				
I never ask questions in class.				
I am scared of reading aloud in class.				
I am scared of being asked a question in class.				
I avoid social situations.				
I prefer to be by myself.				
I hate lunchtimes at school.				
I tend to sit by myself during lunch.				
I often go to the library on my own during lunchtime				
I would like to go to parties but am too afraid.				
I don't like being the centre of attention.				
I get flustered when people talk to me.				
I think I bore other people.				
I don't think I have anything interesting to say.				
I probably blush when anyone speaks to me.				
I am not as interesting to talk to as other children.				

The nearer the score to 20, the more likely it is that your child has a social phobia.

▶ How to treat your child's social phobia

Cognitive approaches using thought-challenging techniques, coupled with social skills training, can be very effective here. Teaching your child to identify and change negative thoughts is very useful, for example:

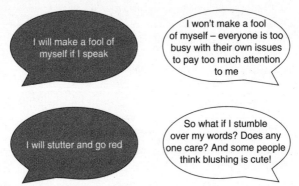

I will make a fool of myself if I speak

I won't make a fool of myself – everyone is too busy with their own issues to pay too much attention to me

I will stutter and go red

So what if I stumble over my words? Does any one care? And some people think blushing is cute!

Write down whatever negative thoughts are feeding your child's anxiety and try to come up with more positive counter-suggestions together. The same distortions in thinking that adults use are often used with children, e.g. exaggeration, or focusing only on the negatives (see Chapter 3). It is probably also worth reading, or rereading, Chapter 6 on adult social phobia.

Key idea

Helping your child to challenge their thoughts about their fears is an essential element of successful treatment of social phobia

As always, a situational hierarchy should be developed to help the young person gradually face their feared situations (see Chapter 4).

SIMPLE PHOBIAS

Whether your child is phobic about lifts, escalators, spiders, buttons, toilets, the dark, thunderstorms, needles, being alone, dogs or clowns (or anything else), in many ways, they should be treated according to the same principles in the rest of this book. Phobias only need treating if they are preventing your child from leading a normal life or are making things hard for your family life.

The programme should always consist of graduated exposure to the feared object or situation (see Chapter 7 for examples with adults). With older children, you can explain about panic attacks and what is happening. You can use logic and reasoned arguments to persuade your older child to cooperate. Younger children, however, are not able to understand that they should not 'escape' – they will not want to face the feared situation at all! Luckily, younger children respond very well to reward systems such as star charts, stickers and prizes. If the prize is desired enough, this system can work well to encourage them to take the steps towards the cure. Even when using rewards, however, steps must be small enough for children to manage and realize that they can cope – if you try to go too fast, no amount of rewards will be worth the anxiety they are experiencing and they will refuse to cooperate.

In order to demonstrate how to apply the techniques outlined in Chapters 4 and 7 to children, an example of choking phobia in children will be used here.

▶ Choking phobia

NB most of this section can also be applied to adults with choking phobia. Choking phobia is not restricted to children (though discussion here will focus on kids). It is characterized by a disproportionate fear of choking on food, tablets or even drinks. Sufferers may avoid food (or have restricted diets) and children may over-chew, hide food or only eat soft foods. Not only does this have consequences for the child's health, but it can also have severe social consequences, as so many social occasions and holidays are centred around food.

Sometimes choking fears can extend to dental phobia and a fear of brushing teeth, but these are often tied in with a hypersensitive gagging reflex too. Choking phobia rarely occurs on its own and in 80 per cent of children with choking phobia (Roos and Jongh, 2008), at least one other psychological disorder is reported, the most common of which are anxiety disorders. Choking phobia in children should also be distinguished from other related conditions (Roos and Jongh, 2008), as summarized in the following table:

Alternative disorder	Characteristics	How choking phobia differs
Extreme gagging reflex	Urge to gag, especially when the back of the mouth is touched. Child might not necessarily be afraid of choking.	Fear of choking is central – there is not usually hypersensitivity to gagging.
Dysphagy	Difficulties swallowing.	Fear of choking is the main fear rather than fear of not being able to swallow.
Globus hystericus	Feeling of lump in the throat. Usually no fear or anxiety.	There is not usually the sensation of a lump in the throat.
Food phobia	Aversion to certain kinds of food that may lead to gagging and urge to vomit.	In choking phobia the anxiety is central (not the gagging or urge to vomit) and isn't linked to any food group.

Child choking phobia questionnaire
How much do you agree with the following statements?

My child is afraid of choking.	Yes = 1	No = 2
My child finds it hard to swallow tablets.	Yes = 1	No = 2
My child seems to have to chew food more than other people.	Yes = 1	No = 2
My child gags when brushing their teeth.	Yes = 2	No = 1
My child avoids the dentist because of their gagging response.	Yes = 2	No = 1
My child seems to have difficulties swallowing.	Yes = 2	No = 1
My child seems worried that they won't be able to swallow food.	Yes = 2	No = 1
My child feels like there is a lump at the back of their throat.	Yes = 2	No = 1
Certain types of food might make my child vomit.	Yes = 2	No = 1
When my child is eating they feel safer to be around other people.	Yes = 1	No = 2

The more '1' responses your child gives, the more likely they are to have a true choking phobia.

Most choking phobias do arise from a direct conditioning response i.e. a traumatic experience with choking. This is why choking phobias differ from many other phobias, which are not always induced by a traumatic experience. Witnessing a choking incident is also a common reason for choking phobia to arise in many children.

How to treat a choking phobia

Many parents (especially mums) are extremely sensitive to their child's eating difficulties and if a phobic child refuses to eat, this can cause panic and distress for parents. Some parents will try to force or pressure the child to eat but this is usually a counter-productive response that will only lead to power struggles between the child and their parents (Roos and Jongh, 2008). Attempting to solve the problem by preparing special food for the child, or by withdrawing the child from school, only makes things worse because this allows the child to avoid the problem and maintains the fear.

Mythbuster

Trying to force your child to eat will not help them with choking phobia

Cognitive behavioural approaches use the techniques summarized below:

- **Relaxation training** Using the techniques in Chapter 3, the child can be taught to relax when attempting to eat food. Do the exercises with your child and show them how to do them. You can also let them feel your own tense and relaxed muscles so that they can feel the difference, and then do the same with their own muscles.

- **Education** This depends on their age. Toddlers or older children can be taught, in an age-appropriate way, the mechanisms of how we eat – the role of saliva, the biology of the trachea etc. – to help them understand what is happening when they eat.

- **Exposure to food** Using the usual situational hierarchies (see Chapter 4), draw up a list of foods in terms of how hard they are for the child to eat. Soft foods will probably be easiest. Using relaxation and praise (see below), encourage your child to move slowly up the hierarchy.

▶ **Positive reinforcement**   Children respond well to praise and reward schemes such as stickers and prizes, so incorporate these into the programme.

Key idea

Gradually exposing your child to different foods can help cure their choking phobia.

Although a simple phobia of choking has been discussed here, the same techniques can be used to tackle almost any simple phobia a child might have (see the case study below and Chapter 7 for more on simple phobias).

Case study: A simple phobia in a child

Emma had a severe button phobia. She was six years old and her fear was so bad that she couldn't wear anything with buttons on it, including her school uniform which, from year 1, included a button-down shirt. She hated even looking at buttons and her mum wasn't 'allowed' to wear any.

I treated this by making it a game with Emma, using a notebook and stickers. First we took her to a supermarket and she chose a lovely fairy notebook and fairy stickers. Then she had to go off with her mum and carry out a task I assigned; her first one was to find an item of clothing with a button on it. If she brought one back to me, she would get a sticker. She managed to do this, holding the shirt out gingerly in her fingers. I asked her to repeat this exercise and after several repetitions (looking for different garments each time) she was holding the clothes quite casually and happily. She was loving the game!

The next session involved trying on clothes in shops. If she was able to try on an item of clothing with a button on it, she got her sticker. She didn't even have to do it up. Once this became easy, she had to have mummy do the buttons up to get her sticker. Once she mastered this game, she was ready to start wearing buttoned clothes at home – for short periods of time at first. She also progressed to allowing mummy to wear clothes with buttons on. By this point, she was able to wear her school shirt with buttons on under her jumper and could cope with getting changed for PE etc.

OBSESSIVE–COMPULSIVE DISORDER

Obsessive-compulsive disorder (OCD) is also fairly common in children, with peak ages being around eight to twelve or adolescence – though children as young as four or five can show symptoms of OCD. With OCD in children, it can be hard to know what is normal childish behaviour and what is not. All children have worries and are often keen on routines, but children with OCD are preoccupied with their worries (obsessions) and these worries compel them to carry out certain ritualistic or repetitive behaviours (compulsions) in order to reduce or cope with these worries. The next chapter explains more about OCD in general and is useful to read in addition to the material here.

Among children with OCD, the most common **obsessions** include:

- fear of dirt or germs;
- fear of contamination;
- a need for symmetry, order and precision;
- a preoccupation with lucky and unlucky numbers;
- fear of illness or harm coming to them or their relatives;
- being bothered by intrusive sounds or words.

These **compulsions** are the most common among children:

- grooming rituals, including hand washing, showering and teeth brushing;
- repeating rituals, including going in and out of doorways, needing to move through spaces in; a special way, or rereading, erasing and rewriting;
- checking rituals to make sure that an appliance is off or a door is locked, and repeatedly checking homework;
- rituals to undo contact with a 'contaminated' person or object;

- touching rituals;
- rituals to prevent harming themselves or others;
- ordering or arranging objects;
- counting rituals;
- hoarding and collecting things of no apparent value or that other people might throw away.

Children often try to involve their parents in their rituals by repeatedly seeking reassurance: e.g. 'Did I count three times?', 'Did I touch that object?' etc. Parents might reassure the child but the relief is only temporary and the child soon seeks reassurance again. If your child spends more than an hour a day engaging in rituals, or continually seeks reassurance, then they may have OCD.

Child OCD questionnaire
How much does your child agree with the following statements?

	1 Strongly agree	2 Somewhat agree	3 Somewhat disagree	4 Strongly disagree
If I touch or go near saliva, urine or sweat I might be harmed.				
I wash my hands many times before I am satisfied.				
I have to repeat a lot of things I do a certain number of times (e.g. three times, seven times etc.).				
If I don't repeat an action a certain number of times, something bad will happen.				
I have to have things in a certain way, e.g. bedding or curtains, otherwise I get very distressed.				
I have to check many times that things are the way I want them before going to sleep/going to school.				
I have to put on my clothes or take them off in a certain order.				

	1 Strongly agree	2 Somewhat agree	3 Somewhat disagree	4 Strongly disagree
I collect unusual things.				
I have to count when I do things.				
I am worried about being around scissors or knives in case I hurt someone with them.				
I check and recheck my homework over and over before handing it in.				
I have to touch some objects a certain number of times when I pass them.				
I can't touch an object that someone else (or a certain person) has touched.				
I get changed many times in the day.				
I need things arranged in a certain order.				
I get upset if other people change the way I have arranged things.				
I repeat certain words or phrases in my mind.				
After I have done something, I need to keep checking that I have really done it.				
There are good and bad numbers.				
I often ask the same question again and again even when it has been answered.				
I have to enter or leave the house, school or classroom in a certain way.				

The more 1s or 2s, the more likely your child is to have OCD (NB this is not a diagnostic tool and not a replacement for a professional diagnosis). Most children won't have all the symptoms listed above and they can change over time.

OCD can be very disruptive because it can prevent the child from getting to school on time, from going on holiday (where routines are different) and even from leaving the house.

Treating OCD in children is not very different from treating it in adults (see Chapter 9), except the programme should be tailored to age-appropriate understanding. Reward schemes (stickers and prizes) etc. work well with younger children, but the key thing to note is not to keep offering unlimited reassurance. Children with severe OCD might need professional input, especially if it is limiting their lives (e.g. ability to attend school).

Mythbuster

Offering repeated reassurance to a child with OCD will only provide very temporary relief, and will make the problem worse rather than better.

A good website for kids is: http://www.ocdkids.org/3.htm. See also Chapter 9 for more on OCD.

Focus points

✳ It is normal for children to have fears and anxieties and these vary by age. If your older child is extremely fearful of things that are more common for a much younger child to be afraid of, or if it is severely limiting their life, there may be cause for concern.

✳ School phobia is a fairly common condition in children but the key to dealing with it is to find the root cause of your child's concerns.

✳ Social phobia occurs in adults and children; many adults first develop this as a child, so nipping it in the bud when they are young can stop it becoming a bigger problem in adulthood.

✳ Children with simple phobias can often be cured by using similar approaches as for adults – except they respond far better to sticker charts and prizes!

✳ Obsessive–compulsive disorder can be an extremely debilitating condition and needs to be treated with particular care. Constantly reassuring your child won't help in the long term.

9

Obsessive–compulsive disorder and post-traumatic stress disorder

In this chapter you will learn:

- *What obsessive–compulsive disorder (OCD) is*
- *About the different types of OCD*
- *What post-traumatic stress disorder (PTSD) is and what causes it*
- *What treatments are available for both disorders*

How do you feel?

1 Do you think obsessively about certain things?   Yes/No

2 Do you feel compelled to repeat certain actions over and over again?   Yes/No

3 Do you worry excessively about things?   Yes/No

4 Have you suffered a traumatic incident that you can't seem to move on from?   Yes/No

5 Do you suffer from flashbacks about a traumatic incident?   Yes/No

A 'Yes' to any of these questions suggests that this chapter will be of particular relevance to you.

OCD (obsessive–compulsive disorder) is a very common anxiety condition and can lead to sufferers being excessively concerned about hygiene, germs, washing or engaging in ritualistic behaviours (such as counting). OCD can take over a person's life, rendering them unable to work, leave the house or engage in normal activities. This chapter discusses the fine line between acceptable concerns and rituals and OCD, before suggesting a treatment programme.

PTSD (post-traumatic stress disorder) can lead to extreme anxiety following a traumatic episode, such as a car accident, that can result in severe panic when faced with feared situations; the second half of this chapter is devoted to this condition.

What is obsessive–compulsive disorder?

Obsessive–compulsive disorder is an anxiety disorder characterized by intrusive thoughts that produce discomfort, apprehension, fear, or worry; the sufferer often performs repetitive behaviours aimed at reducing the associated anxiety. According to OCD-UK, the disorder affects about 1.2 per cent of the population and it can be so debilitating and disabling that the World Health Organization (WHO) has actually ranked OCD in the top ten of the most disabling illnesses in terms of lost earnings and diminished quality of life (http://www.ocduk.org/). OCD is made up of two elements:

▶ **Obsessions** are involuntary, seemingly uncontrollable thoughts, images or impulses that occur over and over again in the sufferer's mind. Sufferers don't want to have these ideas but they can't stop them. These obsessive thoughts are often disturbing and distracting.

Remember this

Obsessions are involuntary so they are not easy to control. Thus, you shouldn't blame yourself if you feel that your obsessions are taking over.

▶ **Compulsions** are behaviours or rituals that the sufferer feels driven to act out repeatedly; often, these compulsions are performed in an attempt to make the obsessions go away or become more manageable. For example, if a person is afraid of contamination with germs and fears catching something, they might develop obsessive hand-washing rituals in order to reduce their on-going worries that they have not washed their hands. However, the relief from washing the hands never lasts and very soon after, another thought will pop into their head – 'Am I sure I washed my hands? Did I wash them properly?' In fact, the obsessive thoughts may even come back stronger. In order to cope with the obsessional thoughts and to reduce the associated anxiety, the hand-washer has to then repeat the hand-washing ritual – and the cycle continues.

Remember this

The relief from carrying out a ritual never lasts long and the sufferer needs to keep repeating it to keep obtaining relief.

Such compulsive behaviours often end up causing anxiety themselves as they become more demanding and time-consuming. If the sufferer fails to 'obey' their thoughts (i.e. by failing to carry out their compulsions), they will also get more and more anxious, leaving them in a no-win situation, trapped by the cycle of obsessions and compulsions.

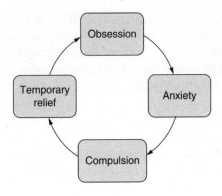

DIFFERENT TYPES OF OCD

Most people with OCD fall into one of the following categories:

▶ **Washers** Afraid of contamination, washers usually have cleaning or hand-washing compulsions. They will often have to repeat the rituals over and over because they are never satisfied that they have done them 'correctly'.

▶ **Checkers** Checkers repeatedly check things (oven turned off, lights are off, door locked, etc.) that they associate with harm or danger. They have to keep checking that they have done something, or else they will obsess about the harm that might result. They may also have to touch things in a certain way, or a certain number of times.

▶ **Perfectors** Perfectors are afraid that if everything isn't perfect or done just right something terrible will happen or they will be punished. Sometimes they have to do things a certain way, like get dressed in a particular order or leave the house in a certain manner.

▶ **Counters and arrangers** This type of OCD sufferer is obsessed with order and symmetry. They may have superstitions about certain numbers, colours or arrangements. They might have to do things a certain number of times and if they don't, or are not sure if they have, they have to start again. Tins in their cupboards may have to be arranged in a certain way (e.g. the labels facing the same way), or clothes hung in their wardrobe must be in certain ritualistic patterns.

▶ **Hoarders** Hoarders fear that something bad will happen if they throw anything away. They compulsively hoard things that they don't need or use, or collect unusual things that other people would throw away.

It is important to note that some people do some of these things but that does not mean they have OCD. Checking that you have locked all the doors three times before you leave the house does not mean you have OCD; checking them 33 times, and being plagued by anxiety even after all this, might. OCD takes over people's lives: it takes up a great deal of time, causes great distress and can stop sufferers carrying out normal day-to-day activities.

Remember this

Lots of people have 'obsessive' tendencies, but this does not mean they have OCD. If your obsessions or compulsions are hindering your ability to lead a normal life, then it's time to take action.

According to Mind (http://www.mind.org.uk/mental_health_a-z/7988_understanding_obsessive–compulsive_disorder_ocd) common obsessions include:

▶ fearing contamination – e.g. from dirt and germs in a toilet;

▶ imagining doing harm – e.g. thinking that you are going to push someone in front of a train;

▶ intrusive sexual impulses – e.g. worrying that you will expose yourself in the street or fondle some stranger;

▶ excessive doubts – e.g. thinking that you have cancer despite having no symptoms;

▶ 'forbidden' thoughts – e.g. thinking about abusing a child;

▶ a fear of failing to prevent harm – e.g. feeling that you are responsible for the safety of others (this can be coupled with an over-inflated sense of responsibility in that you feel you are responsible for the health and safety of people beyond your real control).

It should be noted that these thoughts are not acted upon and that people who have these impulses only fear that they will carry them out, they do not actually do so. It is this dissociation between the thoughts and the reality of their actions that must be learned to break the cycle.

Case study

Wayne was a 38-year-old man who lived alone. His GP referred him to a psychologist but he suffered such severe OCD that he was unable to leave his house. He had many rituals that he was compelled to carry out before leaving his house – such as going up and down the stairs seven times, touching the banister in a certain way, opening and closing the doors in a certain way etc. – and he often had to repeat the whole procedure if he felt he had done something 'wrong'. This meant he could take several hours getting ready to leave. In addition, he was obsessive about germs to the extent that he was too afraid to travel on public transport or go to a public place. As he didn't drive, all his problems meant that a home visit was necessary.

When I turned up, two things struck me at once when he opened the door. Both were connected with his difficulty in actually opening the door – this was because he couldn't bring himself to touch the door handle, so held a handkerchief over it to turn it (which made the handle somewhat slippy). The other issue was that he couldn't open the door fully to let me in because there was a huge pile of mail behind it. I squeezed into the house and asked him about the tottering mountain of mail wedged behind the door. He explained that he couldn't touch the letters because of the germs he feared might be on them. Wayne's hands were also noticeably red raw from repeated washing.

Clearly Wayne was in great need of professional help. His problems were so severe because he had let them build, untreated, for so long. We started by writing down all his rituals and obsessions. We decided to begin the treatment by tackling a ritual – his need to go up and down the stairs seven times every time he came downstairs. I taught him relaxation techniques first and we also discussed the irrational nature of this compulsion. I then encouraged him to go down the stairs just once, then go into the living room to sit down. The first time he did this, he was extremely agitated and anxious – the urge to go back and do it 'right' was almost overwhelming. Using relaxation and talking it through, he managed to sit there until the anxiety went – this took an hour. We repeated this exercise several times over the course of a few weeks until he was comfortable going down the stairs only once. This allowed him to break the obsessive–compulsive pattern and was the breakthrough we needed to tackle his other compulsions.

OCD questionnaire
The following questionnaire is a useful tool to help you examine the type and severity of your OCD.

Tick all those that apply (O = obsession; C = compulsion).

I am afraid of being contaminated by germs or dirt.	O
I am afraid of contaminating others with germs.	O
I am afraid I will harm other people.	O
I am afraid I will harm myself.	O
I am bothered by sexually explicit images.	O
I am bothered by violent thoughts or images.	O
I worry a lot about losing things or not having what I need with me.	O
Everything must be lined up just so.	O
Everything must be arranged in a suitable order.	O
I have a lot of superstitions or things that I must do for luck.	O
I am afraid of shouting something inappropriate out in public (e.g. obscenities).	O
I am always worried that I might have caused an accident while driving.	O
If there is a health scare in the media, I get obsessed that I have the disease or might get it, e.g. swine flu, BSE etc.	O
I have to check that I have locked doors/switched things off etc. many, many times before I can leave the house.	C
I have to check that my loved ones are OK over and over again.	C
I have to count, tap, repeat certain words or do certain rituals in order to reduce my anxiety.	C
I wash my hands repeatedly.	C
My hands are red and chapped from excessive washing.	C
I clean the house far more than most people.	C
I spend a lot of time ordering my things to make sure they are 'just so' and get distressed if someone rearranges them.	C
I pray or carry out other religious rituals excessively.	C
I can't throw anything away.	C
I hoard things that other people would throw away.	C

The more Os ticked, the more obsessions you have; the more Cs ticked, the more compulsions. Often people have both, as the compulsions are carried out in order to cope with the obsessions.

COGNITIVE BEHAVIOURAL THERAPY FOR OCD

Without intervention, OCD rarely goes away on its own. About half of all sufferers will still have OCD after 30 years if they don't have any treatment. Cognitive behavioural therapy for OCD comprises two components:

▶ Exposure and response prevention

This involves repeated exposure to the source of the obsession. Then the sufferer is asked to refrain from the compulsive behaviour that they would usually perform to reduce their anxiety. For example, if you are a compulsive hand washer, you might be asked to touch the door handle in a public toilet and then stop yourself from washing. The anxiety that results from not washing will build up in the same way that any anxiety builds up for phobics when facing the source of their fear – but it WILL decline on its own and of its own accord. This is the key point here; the client has to learn by experiencing it, that the extreme anxiety will gradually reduce on its own. This is because the human brain cannot maintain that level of anxiety for very long and we 'habituate', or get used to, whatever is causing us to be anxious (see Chapter 5).

If the sufferer 'gives in' and washes their hands before the anxiety has subsided, then the cycle is maintained and will not be broken. It is only by having the strength to resist the hand washing that the link will weaken. The trick is to start with something relatively easy, rather than the most difficult thing (see sections on graded exposure and situational hierarchies in Chapter 4).

Key idea

Try not to give in and get the reassurance that you seek as this will just keep the obsessive–compulsive cycle going.

▶ Cognitive therapy

This focuses on the catastrophic thoughts and exaggerated sense of responsibility that sufferers feel. A big part of cognitive therapy for OCD is teaching healthy and effective ways of responding to obsessive thoughts, without resorting to compulsive behaviour. For example, recognizing that the intrusive obsessive thoughts and urges are the result of OCD is an important first step. Then you can replace the thought that 'My hands might be contaminated; I must wash them', with 'I don't think that my hands are contaminated – I'm having an obsession that my hands are contaminated', or 'I'm having a compulsive urge to perform the ritual of washing my hands'.

This would be combined with reminding yourself that nothing bad will happen to you if you don't perform your ritual.

In addition to these two main approaches, the following strategies are also useful:

▶ Stress reduction

The stress and anxiety produced by the obsessions can be managed by stress-reducing strategies. These can also be used as distraction when you are trying to stop yourself carrying out a ritual. The key to success is always trying to break the link between the obsession and the rituals, so that you no longer need to carry out the compulsions. Relaxation therapy (see Chapter 3) can help, as can physical exercise, such as going for a walk or a swim.

▶ Distractions

Do something else to try to stop yourself from carrying out the rituals or thinking about your obsessive thoughts. Activities like watching TV, surfing the web, knitting, exercising, talking with friends, using Facebook etc. can all be distracting enough to weaken the link between the obsessions and the compulsions.

Key idea

Try to find ways of distracting yourself from carrying out your rituals or going over your obsessions.

▶ Write down your obsessive thoughts or worries

Keep a pad and pen with you, or use your phone. When you begin to obsess, write down every one of your thoughts or compulsions. As the OCD urges continue write down everything that is going through your mind, even if you find yourself repeating the same phrases or the same worries over and over. Writing it all down will help you see just how repetitive your obsessions are and help you to break the cycle, plus writing down the same phrase or urge hundreds of times will lessen its power. Writing down all of your thoughts is much harder work and takes far longer than simply thinking them, so your obsessive thoughts are likely to disappear sooner.

▶ Anticipate your OCD tendencies

For example, if you know you have to check that you have turned the oven off, create a list on your phone memo or on a notepad, write the date and note that you have checked the oven (and the time that you did it). This may allow you to transfer your checking to checking your list, rather than checking the actual oven (and could help you leave the house sooner).

▶ Have set worry or OCD times

Rather than trying to stop your obsessions and compulsions, try to limit them to certain times of the day. Allow yourself to write down your worries or carry out your urges but only at these times. At other times, you can jot them down in your notebook, but will have to leave them until the next scheduled 'worry time' (see Chapter 3 for more on this).

Key idea
Writing things down can be a great way to help get on top of OCD behaviour.

▶ Record your worries

Just as writing down your worries over and over can reduce their impact, so can recording them and playing them back to yourself over and over again. You will 'habituate' or get used to the recording and it will no longer produce the same level of distress for you.

▶ Change the status of an obsession

In other words, don't try to make it go away, but change the obsession in some manner. For example, sing your thoughts or make them into a poem. Imagine all your obsessions are a colour and when you think about them, think in that colour.

Please note that severe cases of OCD might benefit from pharmaceutical intervention too so you would need to see your GP. People with severe OCD can sometimes get depressed (see next section) so a visit to the GP is always wise.

An excellent source of advice is OCD-UK: http://www.ocduk.org/

Mythbuster

The family of an OCD sufferer often thinks they are helping by offering reassurance but this can exacerbate the problem and lead to repeated requests for reassurance, none of which bring long-term relief.

A WORD ABOUT POST-NATAL OCD

Post-natal OCD is relatively common, and women who have not previously shown any symptoms of OCD may develop it after the birth of their baby. This is a time when mothers are especially concerned about the health and safety of their precious infant and when they feel totally responsible for their baby's welfare. They may have spent their pregnancy reading about the importance of doing things or not doing them in order to safeguard their baby – e.g. taking folic acid, not smoking or drinking alcohol etc. Therefore, they may feel that if anything were to happen to the baby, it would be their fault. It is also a time of increased stress, a new role and little sleep – all factors that can tip a new mum from being appropriately protective to being unhealthily obsessed with excessive concerns.

According to OCD-UK, common obsessions that occur with post-natal depression include:

- intrusive thoughts of attacking the new baby e.g. by suffocating them;

- unpleasant and intrusive images of throwing or dropping a baby;

- disturbing thoughts of sexually abusing a child;

- fear of accidentally harming a child through carelessness;

- intrusive thoughts of accidentally harming the baby by exposure to medications, chemicals, or certain foods;

- fear of being responsible for giving a child a serious disease such as herpes or AIDS;

- fear of making a wrong decision (i.e. getting inoculations, feeding certain foods, taking anti-depressants) leading to a serious or fatal outcome.

(It should be noted here that having these thoughts does not mean that they will be acted upon or that the baby is necessarily in any real danger.)

This can lead to a number of compulsive rituals including:

- excessive washing of baby clothing;

- avoiding changing soiled nappies for fear of sexually abusing the baby or inadvertently touching them in an inappropriate way;

- excessive washing or sterilizing of the baby's bottles;

- isolating the baby from other people out of fear they might contaminate the baby;

- hiding or throwing out knives, scissors and other sharp objects;

- repeatedly asking family members for reassurance that no harm or abuse has been committed;

- mentally reviewing daily tasks and events in an attempt to get reassurance that they haven't harmed or been responsible for harm to the baby.

It is important to seek help if these symptoms become so overwhelming that you are unable to function normally.

What is post-traumatic stress disorder?

Post-traumatic stress disorder (PTSD) is a severe anxiety disorder that can develop after exposure to any event which results in psychological trauma. This event may involve the threat of death to you or to someone else, or to your own or someone else's physical, sexual or psychological well-being, overwhelming your ability to cope.

The diagnostic criteria for PTSD, stipulated in the *Diagnostic and Statistical Manual of Mental Disorders IV (Text Revision)* (DSM-IV-TR), suggest that in order to be diagnosed with PTSD, the sufferer should:

▶ **Have had exposure to a traumatic event**

This must have involved *both* (a) loss of 'physical integrity', or risk of serious injury or death, to self or others, and (b) a response to the event that involved intense fear, horror, or helplessness (or in children, the response must involve disorganized or agitated behaviour).

▶ **Experience persistent re-experiencing of the event in their mind**

One or more of these must be present in the victim: flashback memories, recurring distressing dreams, subjective re-experiencing of the traumatic event(s), or intense negative psychological or physiological response to any objective or subjective reminder of the traumatic event(s).

▶ **Suffer persistent avoidance and emotional numbing following the event**

This involves a sufficient level of:

▶ avoidance of stimuli associated with the trauma, such as certain thoughts or feelings, or talking about the event(s);

▶ avoidance of behaviours, places, or people that might lead to distressing memories, as well as the disturbing memories, dreams, flashbacks, and intense psychological or physiological distress;

- inability to recall major parts of the trauma(s), or decreased involvement in significant life activities;

- decreased capacity (down to complete inability) to feel certain feelings;

- an expectation that one's future will be somehow constrained in ways not normal to other people.

▶ Experience persistent symptoms of increased arousal not present before

These include difficulty falling or staying asleep, or problems with anger, concentration or hyper-vigilance. Additional symptoms include irritability, angry outbursts, increased startle response, and concentration or sleep problems.

▶ In addition, the symptoms should last for more than one month

If all other criteria are present, but 30 days have not elapsed, the individual is diagnosed with acute stress disorder (which most people would experience immediately after a traumatic event).

▶ The symptoms should also show significant impairment

The symptoms reported must lead to 'clinically significant distress or impairment' of major domains of life activity, such as social relations, occupational activities, or other 'important areas of functioning'.

PTSD is believed to be caused by experiencing any event which produces intense negative feelings of 'fear, helplessness or horror' in the observer or participant. Sources of such feelings may include (but are not limited to):

- military combat (where most research has been carried out);

- serious road accidents;

- terrorist attacks;

- natural disasters, such as severe floods, earthquakes or tsunamis;

- being held hostage;

- witnessing violent deaths;

- violent personal assaults, such as sexual assault, mugging or robbery;

- experiencing or witnessing (in childhood or as an adult) physical, emotional or sexual abuse;

- experiencing or witnessing physical assault, adult experiences of sexual assault, accidents, drug addiction, illnesses, medical complications;

- employment in occupations exposed to war (such as soldiers) or disaster (such as emergency service workers);

- getting a diagnosis of a life-threatening illness.

PTSD can develop immediately after someone experiences a disturbing event or it can occur weeks, months or even years later. PTSD can develop in any situation where a person feels extreme fear, horror or helplessness. However, it doesn't usually develop after situations that are simply upsetting, such as divorce, job loss or failing exams.

It is thought that around a third of people who experience traumatic events will go on to have PTSD. The more disturbing the experience, the more likely you are to develop PTSD. According to the Royal College of Psychiatrists (http://www.rcpsych.ac.uk/expertadvice/problems/ptsd/posttraumaticstressdisorder.aspx) the most traumatic events:

- are sudden and unexpected;

- go on for a long time;

- are when you are trapped and can't get away;

- are man-made;

- cause many deaths;

- cause mutilation and loss of arms or legs;

- involve children.

Mythbuster

PTSD doesn't always occur straight after a traumatic event – it can sometimes take years to develop.

According to NHS Direct (http://www.nhs.uk/conditions/post-traumatic-stress-disorder/pages/introduction.aspx) PTSD affects up to 30 per cent of people who experience a traumatic event. It affects around 5 per cent of men and 10 per cent of women at some point during their life.

PTSD can occur at any age, including during childhood.

Remember this

The symptoms of PTSD must last for more than a month for them to be classified as PTSD. Symptoms within a month of a traumatic incident are normal.

Case study

Richard presented at my clinic with what he claimed to be a phobia about riding his motorbike. It turned out that he had been in quite a serious road traffic accident 18 months previously, in which he had been on his bike and had collided with a car. He had received a number of injuries from which he had recovered, but emotionally, he couldn't get back on a bike. Not only that, he was scared to use any form of transport. He also suffered flashbacks, poor concentration, sleeping difficulties (being woken by nightmares and unable to get back to sleep). He was off work as he was unable to concentrate effectively on his job. He felt anxious all the time and was very 'threat-sensitive' – always on guard for something bad to happen. It was clear that he was suffering from PTSD.

We began treatment by looking at his thoughts and cognitions and by practising relaxation techniques. I also encouraged him to talk about the accident over and over, and to even tape his story and play it back repeatedly, so that it would cease to be so arousing for him. We then started him on public transport which he felt would be easier to tackle than a bike. He was very anxious on the tram but we worked though the anxiety together and challenged his distorted view that it would crash. Once he was comfortable going on the tram with me, he went on it alone a number of times and, gradually, his anxiety began to subside. He began to realize that the tram was unlikely to crash and was able to make longer and longer journeys.

By this point his general anxiety levels were better and he felt able to return to work. However, he decided not to go on a motorbike again, as he realized that motorbikes were probably a less safe form of transport and that an accident could happen again. He decided it was not worth the risk, but was able to function normally by going to work and getting on with his life.

PTSD questionnaire

The following statements refer to the traumatic event that you have been involved with. To what extent do you:

	1 Very much	2 Some what	3 Not very much	4 Not at all
have flashbacks about the event?				
have recurring nightmares?				
try to avoid thinking about it?				
try to avoid anything that reminds you of it?				
find it hard to remember all of what happened?				
have decreased interest in day-to-day life (than before the event)?				
believe that you don't feel things as much as before?				
feel that your life will never be the same as it was before?				
have difficulty falling or staying asleep?				
have difficulty concentrating?				
have many angry outbursts?				

Continued

9. Obsessive–compulsive disorder and post-traumatic stress disorder (209)

	1 Very much	2 Some what	3 Not very much	4 Not at all
often feel irritable?				
feel that you get frightened easily?				
feel 'jumpy'?				
feel that your symptoms impair your ability to work?				
feel that your symptoms impact on your social life?				
feel more aware than before of the dangers or risks in the world?				

The more 1s and 2s you score, the more likely it is that you could have PTSD and might benefit from visiting your GP.

TREATING PTSD

If you think you (or your child) have PTSD the best first point of call is your family doctor. Severe PTSD is very hard to self-treat and professional input is advised. The UK National Centre for Clinical Excellence (NICE) is responsible for providing guidance on treatments and care for those using the NHS in England and Wales. NICE reviews all available treatments for a disorder (both psychological therapies and medication) to establish which are the most effective. The main psychological treatments for post-traumatic stress disorder recommended by NICE, are cognitive behavioural therapy and eye movement desensitization and reprocessing (EMDR).

Remember this

CBT or EMDR are the recommended treatment options for PTSD.

▶ **Eye movement desensitization and reprocessing (EMDR)**

EMDR is a powerful psychological method for treating severe emotional anxiety caused by disturbing life experiences and traumatic events. EMDR was developed by psychologist Dr Francine Shapiro who discovered that eye movements can reduce the intensity of disturbing thoughts under certain circumstances. It seems to work by directly influencing the way that traumatic events are stored in our memory. Traumatic events tend to get 'frozen' in our memory (alongside the feelings and thoughts that go with them) which means they are not processed – so every time we think of them it is as if we are experiencing them for the first time. Flashbacks are the brain's way of trying to process what we say or what happened, but because of the 'freezing' the memories stay as fresh as ever.

EMDR uses a natural function of the body, rapid eye movement (REM), as its basis. The human mind uses REM when we sleep to help it process daily emotional experiences. There is some evidence that the eye movements during EMDR perform a similar function to those that occur during REM sleep (when we dream), which we already know to have a vital information processing function. When trauma is extreme, this process breaks down and REM sleep doesn't bring the usual relief from distress. EMDR is thought to be like an advanced stage of the REM processing. Using eye movement, the brain processes troubling images and feelings, so that resolution of the issue can be achieved.

EMDR requires clients to focus on three main aspects of the trauma: firstly, a visual image which is usually that of the most disturbing part of the trauma; secondly, the negative thought that they have about themselves in relation to the trauma; thirdly, the location of the disturbance in their body.

Focusing on these aspects, the client then tracks the therapist's finger across the visual field in rapid abrupt eye movements (the eye movements can also be created using a 'light bar', in which you follow a light that moves back and forth across a metal bar) and after each set of such movements, the client is simply asked to report on what they are experiencing. During the course of this procedure, a decrease in the emotional impact of the traumatic memory usually occurs. The alternating left–right stimulation of the brain with eye movements, during EMDR, seems to stimulate the frozen or blocked information processing system.

The decrease may be gradual but in some cases may be sudden. The distressing memories seem to lose their intensity, so that the memories are less disturbing and seem more like 'ordinary' memories. EMDR proponents have given a range of explanations for the apparent effectiveness of the lateral eye movements: distraction, relaxation, synchronization of the brain's two hemispheres, and, of course, simulation of the eye movements of rapid eye movement (REM) sleep. But, does it work?

A report in *Scientific American* in 2008 (http://www. scientificamerican.com/article.cfm?id=emdr-taking-a-closer-look) points out that when treating PTSD, EMDR is certainly better than no treatment at all. However, it also claims that traditional CBT (cognitive behavioural therapy) is still proven to be more effective than EMDR.

▶ CBT

A research paper by Kar (2011) reviewed the use of cognitive behavioural therapy for use with PTSD in the following traumatic circumstances: terrorism, war trauma, sexual assault, RTAs (road traffic accidents), refugee status and disaster workers. It found that, in general, CBT was better at achieving longer-lasting results than EMDR, but that in the first three months post-treatment, both were equally as effective. One of the problems with CBT is that the dropout rate is often high, with clients not completing the therapy. This could be because CBT takes longer than EMDR and requires more sessions.

CBT for treating PTSD consists of a number of elements such as:

▶ Psycho-education about common reactions to trauma: this is often a valuable first step as just hearing that their reactions are normal and fit within a syndrome can be very reassuring to clients who fear they are 'going mad'.

▶ Relaxation training: see Chapter 3.

▶ Identification and modification of cognitive distortions: for example, the belief about how dangerous driving appears to be following a car crash.

- ▶ Graduated exposure to avoided situations: e.g. a person who is unable to go in a car following a car crash might start by going on public transport, and graduate only when comfortable to being a passenger in a car (see Chapter 4).

- ▶ Imagined exposure to avoided situations: imagined exposure can be used with relaxation therapy to help the person cope with approaching the real exposure protocol. This is used in the same way as graded exposure (see earlier chapters) except the person imagines doing the tasks rather than actually doing them.

- ▶ Cognitive restructuring: modifying the client's way of thinking and underlying beliefs about themselves, the world at large and how they see the future (see Chapter 10).

- ▶ Guided self-dialogue (positive talk): this involves the development of a personal self-help script that will vary for each client and which can be used in conjunction with graded exposure (see earlier chapters, e.g. Chapter 4)

- ▶ Thought-stopping: learning to stop negative and harmful thoughts in their tracks and replacing them with positive thoughts (see Chapters 3 and 4).

- ▶ Writing about the traumatic incident and re-reading it until it is no longer distressing, or recording the story and playing it back repeatedly.

Key idea

Repeated exposure to the traumatic incident in your mind can help reduce the anxiety associated with it. In time, you will 'habituate' to it and stop being so distressed when thinking of what happened to you.

Many of these elements have been explained and outlined in previous sections of this book. As with EMDR, the intention here is not to train the reader to tackle these therapies themselves, but to explain them so that they might seek the appropriate professional help from a base of knowledge rather than ignorance.

Focus points

❋ OCD is characterized by both obsessions and compulsions, and sufferers may exhibit either one, or both.

❋ There are different types of OCD, such as hoarders and checkers, and sufferers tend to be predominantly one type (though they can be more than one).

❋ OCD sufferers carry out rituals (compulsions) in order to cope with their obsessional thoughts, but these compulsions rarely provide lasting relief.

❋ The only way to gain lasting relief from OCD is to break the cycle of reassurance seeking and learn to cope with the anxiety that this produces.

❋ Post-traumatic stress disorder is a serious anxiety condition that results from being unable to move on from a very traumatic event. The best treatments for this are likely to be cognitive behavioural therapy or eye movement desensitization and reprocessing with trained therapists.

10

Depression

In this chapter you will learn:

▶ *How depression and anxiety are linked*
▶ *About the symptoms of depression*
▶ *About self-esteem and what can cause low self-esteem*
▶ *Techniques for dealing with depression*

How do you feel?

1 Do you think it is your fault that you have an anxiety condition?

Yes/No

2 Do you put yourself down because you can't do certain things?

Yes/No

3 Does having restrictions on what you can do because of your anxiety condition make you depressed?   Yes/No

4 Do you have a lot of negative thoughts about yourself?   Yes/No

5 Do you wish things were different but can't motivate yourself to make any changes?   Yes/No

More 'yes' than 'no' answers to these questions suggests that you might be depressed, have low self-esteem, or both; this chapter is for you.

People who suffer from anxiety conditions can often be prone to depression if their condition begins to seriously impact on their life. Sufferers of social anxiety/phobia or agoraphobia, and OCD are particularly prone to depression, since their lives become more limited; they can no longer go out and enjoy the things they used to. They may also feel worthless and have low self-esteem, because they feel that their anxiety condition is irrational; other people live normal lives, they think, so they feel stupid and inadequate for having these difficulties.

Anxiety–depression link

The initial step, then, in treating depression for clients whose primary problem is an anxiety condition, is reassurance. It is extremely common for clients to make comments to me that clearly reflect their low self-esteem and self-worth in relation to their anxiety condition:

A lot of these thoughts become self-fulfilling prophecies; for example, the more fearful sufferers become of going out, the fewer interesting things they will do, so the less interesting conversation they can make.

No one else is afraid of leaving the house like me – what an idiot I am.

It is stupid to be so afraid of going out – therefore I must be stupid.

I must be very unintelligent to have this need to keep washing my hands.

There is something seriously flawed about me to think the way I do.

Other people my age lead normal lives – my life is rubbish.

I have nothing to say to people – I am really boring.

I can't go out or do much so I am bored and boring.

I don't talk to people because I am so dull.

In addition, people who become more restricted in where they go and what they do, may find that their world becomes smaller and more narrow, so any opportunities for stimulation are lost. Without work, social life and hobbies, it is very easy to become depressed.

Offering reassurance, then, that anxiety conditions can affect everyone and there is nothing silly, stupid or unintelligent about people who suffer from them, is an important first step. Because people tend not to talk about these mental health problems, we often have no idea of who is suffering from them and how common they are. User-groups and chatrooms on the internet can be a good way to find other sufferers and to realize that you are not alone.

Key idea

Joining an internet support group or chatroom can help you realize that you are not the only one with the anxiety condition you are suffering from.

Once the anxiety condition starts to improve, life for the sufferer should also start to improve and the depression should lift. However, for some people, it is the depression associated with the anxiety condition that prevents them from seeking the help they need to overcome the anxiety. So, they do not improve and may deteriorate, leading to further escalation of the depression.

Mythbuster

Anxiety conditions do not discriminate – they affect people from all backgrounds and all levels of intelligence equally.

Case study

Coco had suffered from panic attacks for many years but recently things had got so bad that they began to severely impact her quality of life. She began to be afraid of going on a bus or going into town in case she had an attack. She didn't like being far from home and her world began to get smaller. She didn't drive so being unable to use public transport had a devastating effect on her life. She managed to hold down her job as a PA for a while because a colleague who lived near her used to give her a lift. However, before long she began to panic about getting in the car even with her – what would happen if she had a panic attack, she would think. It would be so embarrassing and difficult to escape from. She became a 'nervous wreck' at work, dreading the journey home. Eventually she was signed off work with stress by her doctor and her world became even smaller.

It wasn't surprising that Coco began to get quite severely depressed. She was a young woman who should have been out clubbing and having fun in the evenings and living a full life, but she couldn't even get to work. Her not going out meant that she stopped seeing people and became used to her own company. She used Facebook and email but it wasn't the same and she found that when friends did come to see her, she found it difficult to think of anything to say – her life seemed so dull compared to theirs. She stopped enjoying life – there was nothing to enjoy. She slept in most days till mid-afternoon and spent the rest of the day slumped in front of the TV.

Her panic attacks had now developed into a bigger problem that was harder to treat. Because of her depression she wasn't motivated to treat the panic attacks – she just couldn't see the point or believe that she would ever get better. So, the starting point had to be to lift her depression enough to begin work on curing her panic attacks.

Depression

Most people feel low or down sometimes, but depression is a far more extreme form of this. Depressed people often have long episodes when they are unable to motivate themselves to do much (even get out of bed), cannot find pleasure in life and feel worthless. There are four main groups of depressive symptoms:

▶ Those to do with feelings, e.g. feeling sad and miserable.

▶ Physical symptoms, e.g. lack of appetite or sleeping difficulties.

▶ Thoughts/cognitions, e.g. 'I am worthless', 'No one likes me'.

▶ Those to do with behaviour, e.g. staying in bed.

Remember this

Depression can affect the way you feel, think and act as well as causing physical symptoms.

Depression questionnaire
How much do you agree with the following statements?

	1 Strongly agree	2 Somewhat agree	3 Somewhat disagree	4 Strongly disagree
I feel extremely sad or upset.				
I am often tearful and weepy.				
I feel lonely.				
I am not motivated to do anything.				
I find it hard to concentrate.				
My appetite has changed – I'm either not hungry or eating too much.				
I feel lethargic and tired.				

Continued

	1 Strongly agree	2 Somewhat agree	3 Somewhat disagree	4 Strongly disagree
I have no energy.				
I sleep too much or too little.				
Nobody likes me.				
I'm a waste of space.				
I always do things wrong.				
Nothing will ever change for me.				
I'm a failure.				
I tend to be on my own a lot.				
I tend to stay in bed a lot.				
There is nothing I enjoy doing.				
I don't do things that I used to enjoy.				
I get tearful easily.				
I can't be bothered to do anything.				
I am unusually irritable or impatient.				
I avoid social events that I used to enjoy.				
I find it hard to make decisions.				
I am to blame for being like this.				
I have no self-confidence.				
I have a lot of negative thoughts.				
I can't see things getting any better for me.				
I think about suicide.*				

*NB If you are in any way suicidal, you should seek professional help. This self-help book will not be enough for very severe depression.

The more 1s you select, the more depressed you might be. Again, severe depression cannot be treated with self-help and should always have input from a professional.

THE CYCLE OF DEPRESSION

Depression is a cycle. When it is anxiety-induced, it often starts with the thoughts/cognitions of worthlessness in connection with the sufferer's phobia/panic attacks/OCD etc. These thoughts of low self-worth (e.g. 'I am stupid to have this condition') lead to feeling down and miserable, which leads to physical symptoms of lethargy etc. These symptoms, feelings and thoughts lead the person to withdraw even more from society than their original condition causes them to – which leads to even more feelings of poor self-worth and so the cycle continues.

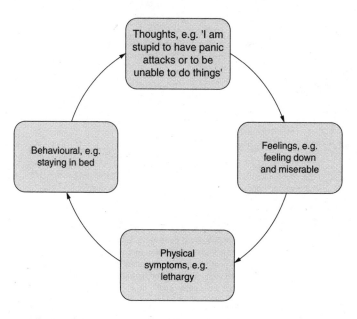

Thoughts, e.g. 'I am stupid to have panic attacks or to be unable to do things'

Feelings, e.g. feeling down and miserable

Physical symptoms, e.g. lethargy

Behavioural, e.g. staying in bed

UNHELPFUL THINKING STYLES

Much of the cycle as outlined above starts and ends with patterns of unhelpful thinking. Many of these unhelpful thinking styles, or cognitive distortions, are the same as with generalized anxiety disorder discussed in Chapter 3. However, instead of the thinking styles leading to anxiety, here they lead to depression.

Unhelpful thinking style	Example related to depression
Predicting the future	Depressed people tend to spend a lot of time thinking about the future and predicting what could go wrong. For example, 'I will fail this exam', 'No one will talk to me at the party', 'I will have a panic attack'. These thoughts can lead to the individual being afraid to try things – 'I will only fail, so what's the point?' – leading to more withdrawal from society and the world, and more depression.
Mind-reading	Here, assumptions are made about what other people are thinking, e.g. 'They must think I am so stupid', 'Everyone will think I am an idiot'. Again, this can prevent the individual from doing things, leading to further negative thoughts and depression.
Catastrophizing	Depressed people often blow things out of all proportion. Things are always 'terrible', rather than just 'not very good'. They also assume that catastrophes will result from minor mistakes, e.g. 'I was late meeting a friend – they will never want to meet me again'. These thoughts lead to further negative self-evaluations ('I really blew it – what an idiot I am') and add to the depression.
Taking things personally	A classic example of this is with the weather: 'It always rains when I go out' or 'Typical, someone up there must really hate me'. Or the depressed individual takes some minor incident personally, e.g. a colleague is quiet at work so they assume they must have offended them. This adds to their own feelings of poor self-esteem, thus feeding the depression.
Should-ing	'Should' statements are commonly used by depressed people to refer to how badly things have gone and to take the blame for what happened, e.g. 'I should have done this or that'. All this serves to make the person feel even worse about themselves and adds to their depressed state.
Over-generalizing	This is where one incident that didn't go well leads to the assumption that everything else will follow a similar pattern. Non-depressed people can shrug off things going wrong, but depressed people will assume that if they did poorly on one thing, they will perform poorly at everything else. For example, if they stumbled over their words in a shop, they assume they will always lack the ability to communicate well.
Black-and-white thinking	When people are depressed, they often see things as either black or white with no shades of grey in between. For example, they either did something perfectly or terribly – and, as perfection is rare, this only serves to feed into their depression.
Ignoring the positives	Depressed people often ignore or don't notice when things go well and only focus on when things go badly. For example, if they are at a social event, they might ignore the fact that eight people smiled at them, and only focus on the one person who ignored them.
Labelling	Finally, depressed people are more likely to label themselves as 'rubbish', 'a failure', 'boring' etc. Labelling like this can add to their feelings of poor self-worth.

Key idea

Identifying unhelpful patterns of thinking can be an important step in beating depression.

▶ Thought-catching exercise

Write down your unhelpful thoughts as they occur within the following categories:

Unhelpful thinking style	Example
Predicting the future	
Mind-reading	
Catastrophizing	
Taking things personally	
Should-ing	
Over-generalizing	
Black-and-white thinking	
Ignoring the positives	
Labelling	

▶ Challenging unhelpful thoughts

Once you have identified your unhelpful thoughts, you then need to start challenging them. You can do this with the following question sequence:

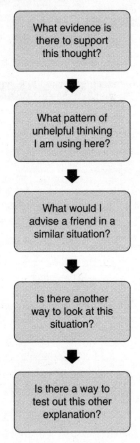

What evidence is there to support this thought?

⬇

What pattern of unhelpful thinking I am using here?

⬇

What would I advise a friend in a similar situation?

⬇

Is there another way to look at this situation?

⬇

Is there a way to test out this other explanation?

This can lead to the idea of 'hypothesis testing', whereby the individual comes up with a possible alternative way of thinking that is more helpful, and then tests it out (see also Chapter 3 on challenging unhelpful thoughts in relation to anxiety conditions).

Example

Jane is at a party where Joanne appears to ignore her. Jane is devastated by this, even though several other people have spoken to her. She decides that she is boring and ugly and this is why Joanne ignored her. She leaves the party and goes home miserable.

What evidence is there to support the thought that she is boring and ugly?
In reality, none. No one has actually told her this. There could be lots of reason why Joanne didn't speak to Jane.

What patterns of unhelpful thinking is she using?
Mind-reading, taking things personally, labelling, ignoring the positives.

What would she advise a friend?
Most likely she would point out the several people who did speak to her, so she can't be as ugly and boring as she imagined!

Is there another way to look at the situation?
Perhaps Joanne was distracted or maybe she didn't even see Jane!

Can this hypothesis be tested out?
Jane could get someone to ask Joanne if she was deliberately ignoring her.

LOOKING FOR PLEASURE IN LIFE

Depressed people stop enjoying the things they used to enjoy. They 'can't be bothered' to pursue their hobbies and interests, or maybe are prevented from doing so by their anxiety condition. Part of overcoming depression is learning to find pleasure in the simple things again. This means looking for things that you can appreciate, which bring you pleasure or which you can enjoy. You should look for three such things every day – they can be as small as enjoying a cup of coffee, or smelling newly-mown grass, or bigger things like going to the seaside or playing sport. The possibilities are endless! See below for inspiration.

Mythbuster

It isn't always the big things in life that we need to feel happy – the little things can help lift our mood on a daily basis.

Activity	How much did you enjoy before (0–100)?
Having a long, hot bath	
Collecting things	
Playing an instrument	
Playing a team sport	
Swimming	
Going for a walk	
Chatting to a friend	
Coffee	
A meal out	
Coffee and a cake with a friend	
Going to a party or social event	
The smell of freshly-mown grass	
Walking in the sunshine	
Going to a cinema	
Watching TV	
Reading a book/magazine	
Shopping	
Stroking a pet	
Walking a dog	
Watching children play	
Playing with your own children	
Baking/cooking	
Gardening	
Being creative (e.g. making jewellery)	
Painting/drawing	
Listening to music	
Writing stories	
Looking at old photos	
Taking photos	
Meeting new people	
Seeing nice scenery	
Repairing things	
Being with the family	
Sex	

Singing	
Going to a religious activity/service	
Feeling the sand between your toes	
Seeing animals	
Ice-skating/roller-skating	
Travelling	
Having people round	
Buying a gift for someone	
Sightseeing	
Having beauty treatments	
Eating	
Going on social networking sites	
Surfing the web	
Star-gazing	
Acting	
Being alone	
Dancing	
Having a day out with the children	
Having a picnic	
Doing crosswords or sudoku (or similar)	
Going to a museum or art gallery	
Volunteering in the community	
Doing jigsaws	
Having a hot chocolate	
Eating an ice cream	
Going to a park	
Watching ducks in water	
Watching a sunset	
Seeing the first blossom of spring	
Standing in the snow	
Building a snowman	
Sledging with the children	
Add your own here:	

Establishing a daily schedule is an important part of lifting yourself out of depression. Try to build some of the activities that you have identified above, which you enjoyed in the past, into your daily schedule.

Key idea

Looking for simple pleasures in life and scheduling them into your daily routine can really help lift you out of depression.

Core beliefs

So far, we have looked at how to challenge and change unhelpful or distorted thinking that can lead to feeling down or depressed, as well as suggesting ways to look for pleasure and enjoyment in life. Sometimes, however, people are hampered by being rooted in very strong ways of thinking that prove hard to change. Psychologists sometimes call these 'core beliefs' and they describe the very essence of how we view ourselves, our world, our future and other people. These core beliefs are often activated or switched on in certain situations – for example, some people find that they always get depressed after visiting their parents or a certain friend; this is usually because the visit has activated some core belief that they hold. Examples of core beliefs are summarized in the table below:

Core beliefs about myself	Core beliefs about other people	Core beliefs about my future	Core beliefs about the world
I am stupid.	Everyone else is cleverer than me.	Nothing good ever happens to me.	The world is a cruel place.
I am not likeable.	Everyone else is likeable.	I won't ever have friends.	The world is an unfriendly place.
I get everything wrong.	Other people get everything right.	I will never get anything right.	The world is too complicated.

Core beliefs often develop in childhood or through significant life events. They are strong beliefs that are often rigidly held, even in the face of conflicting evidence. Thus, the cognitive distortions discussed earlier in the chapter allow people to dismiss any evidence that they are likeable, do have friends etc., and allow their core beliefs to be reinforced. Not surprisingly, this has a clear impact on their self-esteem and feelings of self-worth.

IDENTIFYING AND CHALLENGING YOUR CORE BELIEFS

It is useful then to identify and try to challenge any core beliefs that might be holding back progress at this point. Firstly, identify your core beliefs (CB) – you can add to this list later on:

Core beliefs that I hold:
1.
2.
3.
4.
5.
6.

Key idea

Identifying and challenging the core beliefs that have contributed to your depression and low self-esteem over the years is a valuable learning experience.

Next, select each CB in turn, and look for evidence that might contradict this. For example:

CB: I am stupid

Counter evidence:
* I got five good 'O Levels'.
* I completed a secretarial course.
* I passed my driving test first time.
* I held down a good job before I had kids.

Now, rewrite your CB:
* New CB: I might not be a great intellect, but I am definitely not stupid!

Sometimes, you can test your CBs to see if they are true. For example, in order to test if you really are 'stupid', take an IQ test, read an 'intelligent' book (and see if you enjoy it), or enrol on a study course. If your CB is that no one likes you, try smiling at acquaintances and seeing if they smile back, or even inviting someone out for a coffee.

Testing CBs: An example

Janice's CB was that 'no one likes me' and this was the source of her depression. She was convinced that everyone ignored her, both in real life and on Facebook. Consequently, she had stopped talking to people, and walked around with her eyes to the ground. She stopped posting on FB too.

As an experiment, she decided to smile and say hello to ten people she was vaguely friendly with and note their response. To her surprise nine out of ten smiled back! Five engaged her in small talk, and during this, Janice plucked up the courage to suggest meeting for a coffee. Consequently, she met up with three of them, and was forced to conclude that her CB may have been wrong. She also started posting again on FB and noted that two out of five posts got some responses. She noticed too that a lot of posts from other people often seemed to be 'ignored' too, and concluded that she might not be as unpopular as she first thought.

Self-esteem

Not everyone who has a phobia or panic disorder has low self-esteem at all; in fact, many of my clients are probably quite healthy in that department! However, I have yet to come across anyone who is depressed who has a high self-esteem. It is probable that the panic or anxiety disorder leads to lowered self-esteem which in turn leads to the depression.

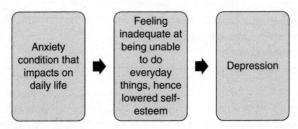

What do we mean by 'self-esteem'? Self-esteem refers to how we feel about ourselves – the value or worth that we feel we have. Someone with high self-esteem will like themselves, be aware of what they are good at and accepting of the things they are less good at. Someone with low self-esteem, on the other hand, does not like themselves, believes that they are good at very few things and tends to over-focus on the things that they are bad at. Self-esteem differs slightly from self-confidence which refers more to our ability to do something rather than our overall sense of self-worth. For example, I have poor self-confidence in my ability to sing in tune (sadly!), but don't believe that this makes me a 'rubbish' or unworthy person.

Symptoms of low self-esteem include:

▶ Unfavourable comparisons with other people.

▶ Lack of acknowledgement of positive qualities/achievements.

▶ Distorted thinking, e.g. 'I must be perfect', 'I must not make mistakes', 'I must be good company' etc.

▶ Unrealistic understanding of how much other people scrutinize you.

▶ Over-concern with other people's judgements.

▶ Inability to let go of 'failures'.

▶ Allowing other people to control you.

▶ Blaming yourself for things going wrong.

TWO KINDS OF SELF-ESTEEM

Psychologists recognize two types of self-esteem (SE): global and situational.

▶ **Global SE.** This is the fairly constant view that we have of our self-worth and tends to be quite stable over time. Global SE is about who we are.

▶ **Situational SE.** This, on the other hand, is more variable and relates to specific situations. It is thus more about what we are doing than who we are. For example, a person might have low SE at home but a much higher SE at work. Or they may have poor SE when it comes to IT or computer work, but a higher SE when it comes to writing reports. Situational SE is more akin to self-confidence than Global SE is.

Remember this

There are two kinds of self-esteem: global and situational. Global self-esteem is much more resistant to change.

Self-esteem questionnaire
How much do you agree with the following statements?

	1 Strongly agree	2 Somewhat agree	3 Somewhat disagree	4 Strongly disagree
I don't like myself.				
I consider myself to be unattractive compared with most other people my age.				
I wish I looked different.				
I often wish I were someone else.				
There are many things about myself that I would change if I could.				
I find it hard to make decisions.				
If make a choice I usually believe I made the wrong choice.				
I am not much fun to be around.				
I am boring.				
I usually do the wrong thing.				
I rarely do anything that makes me feel proud of myself.				
I don't think I have achieved much in my life.				
I don't have many good qualities.				
I am not really good at anything useful or worthy.				

The lower your score (the nearer to 14), the lower your self-esteem and the more this is likely to lead to your feeling depressed.

RAISING YOUR SELF-ESTEEM
Raising your self-esteem can have a positive impact on your low mood and depression. One way to do this is to make 'What's good about me' lists' (see below).

Try it now: 'What's good about me' lists

Making lists, rereading them often, and rewriting them from time to time will help you to feel better about yourself. If you find this difficult to do on your own, find a trusted friend to help you.

Make a list of:
* At least five of your strengths, such as persistence, courage, friendliness, or creativity.
* At least five things you admire about yourself, such as the way you have raised your children, your good relationship with your brother, or your spirituality.
* The five greatest achievements in your life so far, like recovering from a serious illness, graduating from high school, or learning to use a computer.
* At least 20 accomplishments – they can range from something as simple as going to the shops by yourself to getting an advanced college degree.
* Ten things you could do to help someone else.
* Ten things you do that make you feel good about yourself.

Case study

Sammy was a pleasant young man who was a social worker, but suffering from very low self-esteem. It turned out that he had been badly bullied at school for a long time and this had severely affected his sense of self-worth. He found it hard to make friends because of this – he felt everyone else was better than him. This made him feel quite depressed and was starting to affect his work.

When he tried to make his 'What's good about me' lists, he really struggled. I had to prompt him to come up with positive things to say about himself. I asked him how a friend would describe him, what grades he had achieved at school, whether he had attended any clubs, studied any instruments, ever received a compliment etc. I encouraged him to ask his family and the few close friends he had too. Eventually he came up with his lists and they contained so much amazing stuff: great A-Level grades, an award for Maths at school, Grade 5 on the trumpet, teaching his grandfather to use a computer...all kinds of things that helped him realize the many good qualities he had.

Another way to do the above exercise is to answer more specific questions in the form of the following template:

What things do you do well?	
What have you achieved in your life?	
What have you done that was hard to do?	
What things do you know a lot about?	
What things can you do easily or quickly?	
Is there any evidence that shows you are good at something?	
What things have people thanked you for?	
When have you been helpful to others?	
What evidence is there that people like you?	
What compliments have you been given?	
What positive qualities do you have?	
Is there anything at all that shows you are appreciated?	
When have people been nice to you or done you a favour?	

Again, it can be very useful to have someone else help you with this exercise; in fact, a very effective technique is to have a trusted friend complete it first (in respect to you) and then you to complete your version separately, then compare. When we are feeling down and depressed, it can be hard to think of positive things about ourselves, so enlisting the help of others can be very useful.

A FINAL WORD ABOUT SELF-ESTEEM AND PANIC ATTACKS

Panic attack sufferers, and sometimes phobia sufferers too, often have low self-esteem because they feel that only 'stupid' people have the condition that they have. They look at 'everyone else' and compare themselves unfavourably, because others appear to be able to do simple, ordinary things that are beyond their reach. This leads to lower and lower feelings of self-worth which in turn can lead to depression.

Thus, it is important to remember that PAs and phobias do not strike 'stupid' people. In fact, they are non-discriminatory, as the first two chapters of this book have illustrated. Educated and clever people with important, high-powered jobs and careers are as likely to suffer from panic attacks and phobias as anyone else. Once you have the condition (and remember, it can come out of the blue for no apparent reason at all), it is easy to let it gradually restrict your life. This is not because of any mental deficits at all – the condition impacts just as much on the highly intelligent as the less so. Therefore, to feel 'stupid' is just plain wrong, and part of the process of building self-esteem is to challenge your thinking and to knock down your 'self-critic'. We would be highly unlikely to regard a friend with the condition as stupid or worthless, so why are we so hard on ourselves?

We have to:

- be kinder to ourselves;
- become less self-critical;
- be more forgiving of our mistakes;
- become more aware of things we have done well or are doing well;
- congratulate ourselves on small achievements (like leaving the house, or facing our fears);
- treat ourselves as we would treat our friends;
- accept our phobia/panic Attacks/OCD etc. without seeing them as a slight on our worthiness or value as an individual.

Remember this

Having panic attacks, OCD, phobias or other anxiety conditions does not make you a less worthy person than anyone else, any more than having any kind of physical illness would.

Only by achieving the above, can you really start to build your self-esteem, tackle your depression and feel good about yourself, whether or not your anxiety condition is still an issue. As your panic attacks etc. become more controlled (through the techniques in this book), your self-esteem should also build, but working on both areas simultaneously can produce a more effective result of a happier, less anxious you!

Focus points

* Many highly intelligent people who hold down high-powered jobs suffer from anxiety conditions, so there should be no shame or feelings of inadequacy about having such a condition.
* Most people who are depressed think in unhelpful or distorted ways; identifying and then challenging these 'thinking errors' can be very helpful.
* We all have 'core beliefs' about ourselves, our world, our future and about other people. Some of these beliefs are unhelpful and can make us feel more depressed, so identifying and challenging these (by looking for evidence) is useful.
* People with low self-esteem tend to make very negative judgements about themselves and find it difficult to find much good in themselves. The exercises in this chapter are designed to challenge these beliefs by identifying as many categories of attributes that are positive.
* People with low self-esteem are often nicer to others than they are to themselves so in order to raise self-esteem, they need to be kind to themselves and treat themselves as they would treat their friends.

Further reading

CHAPTER 1

Adler, J M and Cook-Nobles, R (2011) 'The successful treatment of specific phobia in a college counseling center' *Journal of College Student Psychotherapy* **25**, pp 56–66

Coelho C M and Purkis H (2009) 'The origins of specific phobias: influential theories and current perspectives' *Review of General Psychology* (**13**) **no 4**, pp 335–48

Greenberg D, Stravynski A and Bilu Y (2004) 'Social phobia in ultra-orthodox Jewish males: culture-bound syndrome or virtue?' *Mental Health, Religion and Culture* 7, pp 289–305

Grenier S, Scuurmans J, Goldfarb M, Preville M, Boyer R, O'Connor K, Potvin O and Hudon C (2011) 'The epidemiology of specific phobia and subthreshold fear subtypes in a community-based sample of older adults' *Depression and Anxiety* **28** pp 456–63

CHAPTER 2

Austin D W and Richards J C (2006) 'A test of core assumptions of the catastrophic misinterpretation model of panic disorder' *Cognitive Theory and Research* **vol 30 (1)** pp 53–68

Craske M G, Kircanski K, Epstein A, Wittchen H, Pine D S, Lewis-Fernandez R, Hinton D (2010) 'Panic disorder: a review of DSM-IV; Panic disorder and proposals for DSM-V' *Depression and Anxiety* **27** pp 93–112

Kircanski K, Craske M G, Epstein A M and Wittchen H (2009) 'Subtypes of panic attacks: a critical review of the empirical literature' *Depression and Anxiety* **26** pp 878–87

Raffa S D, White K S and Barlow D H (2004) 'Feared consequences of panic attacks in panic disorder: a qualitative and quantitative analysis' *Cognitive Behavioural Therapy* **33 (4)** pp 199–207

Roth W T, Wilhelm F H and Pettit D (2005) 'Are current theories of panic falsifiable?' *Psychological Bulletin* **131**, pp 171–92

Teng E J, Chaison A D, Bailey S D, Hamilton J D and Dunn N J (2008) 'When anxiety symptoms masquerade as medical symptoms: what medical specialists know about panic disorder and available psychological treatments' *Journal of Clinical Psychological Medical Settings*, **15**, pp 314–31

CHAPTER 4

Sketchley-Kaye K, Jenks R, Miles C and Johnson A J (2011) 'Chewing gum modifies state anxiety and alertness under conditions of social stress' *Nutritional Neuroscience* **Vol 14 (6)** pp 237–42

CHAPTER 5

Tindall, Blaire 'Playing better through chemistry' *The New York Times* 17 October 2004

CHAPTER 6

Burns D D (1989) *The feeling good handbook: using the new mood therapy in everyday life* (New York: W Morrow)

Burstein M, Ameli-Grillon L and Merikangas K R (2011) 'Shyness versus social phobia in US youth' *Pediatrics* **128 (5)** pp 917–25

Iketani T, et al (2002) 'Relationship between perfectionism and agoraphobia' *Cognitive Behavioural Therapy* **Vol 31 (3)** pp 119–28

Perugi, Frare and Toni (2007) 'Diagnosis and treatment of agoraphobia with panic disorder' *Therapy in Practice* **21 (9)** pp 741–64

Pet J, Hougaard E, Hecksher M S and Rosenberg N K (2010) 'A randomized pilot study of mindfulness-based cognitive therapy and group cognitive-behavioural therapy for young adults with social phobia' *Scandinavian Journal of Psychology* **51**, pp 403–10

Veale D (2003) 'Treatment of Social Phobia' *Advances in Psychiatric Treatment* **9**, pp 258–64

CHAPTER 7

Accurso, V, et al (August 2001) 'Predisposition to Vasovagal Syncope in Subjects With Blood/Injury Phobia' *Circulation* **104 (8)** pp 903–7

Boffino, C C, Cardoso, de Sa C S, Gorenstein, C and Brown, R C (2009) 'Fear of heights: cognitive performance and postural control' *Eur Arch Psychiatry Clin Neuroscience* **259**, pp 114–19

Davidson A L, Boyle C and Lauchlan F (2008) 'Scared to lose control? General and health locus of control in females with a phobia of vomiting' *Journal of Clinical Psychology* **64(1)** pp 30–9

Depla, Marja F I A, Have, M L, van Balkom, A J I M (2008) 'Specific fears and phobias in the general population: results from the Netherlands Mental Health Survey and Incidence Study (NEMESIS)' *Soc. Psychiatry Epidermiol* **43** pp 200–8

Hoffman and Human (2003) 'Experiences, characteristics and treatment of women suffering from dog phobia' *Anthrozoos* **16** p 91

CHAPTER 8

Chitiyo M and Wheeler J J (2006) 'School phobia: understanding a complex behavioural response' *Journal of Research in Special Educational Needs*, **Vol 6 (2)** pp 87–91

King N J and Ollendick T H (1997) 'Annotation: treatment of childhood phobias' *J Child Psychol and Psychiatry* **38 (4)** pp 389–400

Roos C and Jongh A (2008) 'EMDR Treatment of children and adolescents with a choking phobia' *Journal of EMDR Practice and Research* **(2) no 3** pp 201–11

CHAPTER 9

Kar, N (2011) 'Cognitive behavioral therapy for the treatment of post-traumatic stress disorder: a review' *Neuropsychiatr Dis Treat* **7** pp 167–81

Index